TOUCHING BASE

52 Devotions to Connect with Your Spouse

SHERMAN & TAMMY ATEN

with Contributions from Aten Ministries Board of Directors

WHAT PEOPLE ARE SAYING

Sherman and Tammy Aten have invested their lives in strengthening believers and churches worldwide. They have invested their lives in building a strong, Christ-centered marriage and family. Now, they extend that ministry to other couples through *Touching Base*. Sherman and Tammy are the real deal. Your life and marriage will be enriched through their practical insights and encouragement.

Michael D. Dean, Lead Teaching Pastor (retired),
Travis Avenue Baptist Church, Fort Worth, Texas

This devotional is filled with stories that ultimately glorify our Lord. I wholeheartedly recommend this book because their heart is to see others within the body of Christ to be encouraged and, more importantly, to make much of Christ.

Michael O'Brien, Singer and Songwriter

Touching Base expresses the heart of God's word, applying it to your life. Sherman & Tammy have woven together 52 devotions to enhance every relationship; it will inspire, encourage, and lead you to its very source—the Living Word, Jesus.

Stephen Richardson, Lead Pastor, All Nations Church,
Carvoeiro, Portugal

Touching Base packs a powerful punch through the lens called life! It takes us through the twists and turns we go through daily with raw honesty and practical wisdom. This book challenges the reader to seek God with every decision and doubt.

Tammy Whitehurst, Speaker and Author

Get ready to enrich your marriage journey with *Touching Base*. Each devotional is a guiding light, providing a source of reflection and growth for couples to share throughout the year. This book beautifully encapsulates the essence of togetherness, fostering a deeper connection between spouses and strengthening their bond. Let these weekly devotionals be your companion on the path to a stronger, more fulfilling marriage.

Aurora de Rodriguez, International Program Director, Global Children's Network, Portugal

The Atens have been faithful and effective servants in the work of the Lord for a generation. And now God has opened a new door of ministry for them—a devotional guide featuring things God has shown them across the years. Their ministry together has been an excellent example in all the churches. Oh, how our families need what they are sharing!

D. L. Lowrie, Pastor Emeritus, First Baptist Church, Lubbock

Praying with your spouse is the most significant investment you can make in your married life—a real challenge for many couples. In *Touching Base,* you'll find simple tools to develop the habit of setting aside time to hold hands and pray together as husband and wife. Following God alone is very difficult. Yet praying together as a couple not only encourages each other, but the presence of God Himself strengthens us. One alone can be overcome, but being together can resist. The three-stranded rope is not easily broken!

Elias Jose Hernandez Olivet & Eglee Bolivar De Hernandez, Pastors, El Amor De Dios Baptist Church, Coro, Falcon, Venezuela

We were deeply moved by the wisdom and guidance this book offers. It combines practical advice with spiritual insights, helping couples strengthen their bond, grow in love, and nurture their faith together.

Mr. & Mrs. Shehrazer Dawood, Principal, St. Thomas Christian High School, Lahore, Pakistan

The focus of these weekly devotionals is Jesus Christ and how He works in our lives as a prophet, priest, and king, particularly in marriages.

Touching Base is a collection of well-written devotionals with important messages for adults, parents, and friends who walk together. For those of us married, in these days of divorce, troubles with sexual orientation, and breakdown of the nuclear family, God needs to be the "third strand" of the rope or union formed when a man and a woman join in holy matrimony. This book will help us to remember the "journey is the destination."

Colonel James Lenard, USMC (Retired)

This magnificent book will enrich and build many people's lives, marriages, and families. It transmits life—with real experiences—that will bless your life if put into action.

Pastor Lucas Medina, The Father of Baptist works in Falcon, Coro, Venezuela

Touching Base concentrates on the wonderful practical experience of many married couples who went through difficult trials in life and their relationship but did not lose hope in God. On every page, you can see the focus on God, His closeness to us, and His sincere interest in building a happy Christian family.

Sergii Syzonenko, Senior Pastor Central Baptist Church, Dnipro, Ukraine

The book's weekly readings seamlessly blend biblical wisdom and practical insights, fostering deeper connection and communication between spouses. Its understandable language and relatable experiences, combined with thought-provoking questions, will spark discussion for couples committed to nurturing and strengthening their relationship and faith within the framework of Christian marriage.

Dr. Bobby Hall, President, Wayland Baptist University

Kindness, understanding, and a shepherd's heart are the things that come to mind when I think of Sherman and Tammy Aten. Throughout this book, enjoy a look at couples who sought to advance the Gospel through their lives, no matter the circumstances or restrictions. Read and be blessed!

Zack Randles, Lead Pastor Waterfront Church, Washington, D.C.

Each devotional speaks of God's Truth at work in real-life situations. Reading about how His truth works in the life of a fellow believer helps me clearly see how that truth can work in my life. God's truth never changes, and His truth can always change a heart that desires to hear. You will be blessed and changed by the truth of God in the devotions contained in *Touching Base*.

Rodney Cavett, President Emeritus, International Commission

Sherman and Tammy do not shy away from addressing these difficulties while simultaneously delivering hope through the Word of God. The stories in this book reveal the realities of couples' lives and encourage us to view life through the lens of God's word. By engaging in these devotionals, your family will be blessed with God's hope and wisdom.

Rui Sabino, Pastor, Baptist Church of Queluz and
President, Portuguese Baptist Convention

Touching Base is an important devotional for couples that desire not just to survive but to thrive in their marriage. It's extremely helpful that each chapter ends with challenges and topics to be discussed with your spouse. There are many useful marriage books and devotionals. Still, this one is extra special because it is not just to be read but to be prayerfully worked through together.

Rusty Ford, IMB Missionary, Spain

Ordering Information: Special discounts are available on quantity purchases by churches, associations, and others. For details, please contact the author at the address listed at the back of the book.

Touching Base—1st ed.

ISBN: 978-1-961641-04-4

Printed in The United States of America

CONTENTS

DEDICATION

Tammy and I want to give a strong and courageous charge—as a captain to his soldiers—in the dedication of this book. Our charge is to those equipped to carry our legacy to the next generation and beyond—our son and daughter, Josh and Brooke.

*And with great expectations, this charge is also to the **children of all our authors/contributors**. May they take the truths we have lived before them and remind the world of the beauty of marriage and family, done God's way!*

To
Pamela, Kimberly, Kristen,
Hailey, Tanner,
Michelle, Daniel, Stephen, Esther, Christopher, Jonathan,
Jennifer, Alyssa, Brianna,
Robert John, Ryan, Sarah,
Brandon,
Mindy, Dalese, Donna,
Zack, Sam, Hayley,
Jason, Steven, Warren, Marina, Christian, Tori,
and Kinna Blair,
we dedicate this book to you.

FOREWORD

ONCE IN A WHILE, you meet someone special who captures your heart significantly. That happened to us when we shared the leadership of a church revival in East Texas several years ago with Sherman and Tammy. They are talented musicians and easily connected to the many teenagers and even older adults who came for those services.

But what impressed us the most was that they are *real* people with a *real* ministry. They have been serving the Lord for decades, and their versatility and flexibility are remarkable. Sherman and Tammy are talented musicians and share the Gospel worldwide.

They appeal to all believers but focus on helping those in Gospel ministry to strengthen their own lives and marriages. We shared one of those marriage retreats in Granbury, Texas, some years ago, and each year, they explore new opportunities in countries worldwide.

Their ministry has impacted ministers and wives in places like Pakistan, Turkey, Ukraine, Spain, Portugal, Aruba, the Philippines, Venezuela, and across the United States. The Atens can communicate God's truths in our country and different countries, especially in places where the Gospel is not widely known. Their ministry stands out because they lead by example and live according to their teachings. You can't beat that; they are the real deal!

These pages are cherished biblical truths presented in a compelling, believable, and effective way. The intention isn't to pressure readers with these messages. Practically and biblically, these pages are written with passion and compassion.

Sherman and Tammy are a couple who love each other and love Jesus and are dedicated to serving wherever God leads them. The pages before you are the results of their years of ministry, along with the board of directors of their ministry. Read them and be blessed. Apply the truths in these pages, and your life and marriage will be transformed. We are so excited to introduce this remarkable book to you.

—Jimmy & Carol Ann Draper, President Emeritus,

LifeWay Christian

INTRODUCTION

IN 2020, we spent a lot of time sitting, thinking, cleaning out stuff . . . all while processing this new experience of a pandemic. We were to have traveled to Pakistan with our friends, Scott & Lori Dix, for a Christian marriage conference the first week of March. I have been to Pakistan several times, but this would be the first time with our wives. Our visas, however, kept being denied, with no explanation. Hmmm. I was bumfuzzled.

I wish God had given me some hint that this trip wasn't going to happen, so I wouldn't have spent my days & His dollars trying to make it happen. But if it had! Oh, what God saved us from! We would have been stuck in Heaven knows where, somewhere between Texas & the Middle East, with our precious wives as the world began to shut down.

20/20 hindsight! (2020. Get it?) Oh well!

Thus began the cancellation of the next three months of our ministry schedule. *Wow! What is happening? And how will we do this financially, mentally, emotionally, and physically?*

I began to analyze every area of my life: ministry, family & friends. What a journey we had been on as a family that started on Thanksgiving Day in November 1990. God birthed Aten Ministries through Henry Blackaby's writing of *Experiencing God*. Dr. Blackaby came to our church in Artesia, New Mexico, where I served on staff and did what he always does—simply shared what God was doing and how we could join Him in His work.

As a couple in our late 20s, we began to pray for God to show us where He was working. And He did! Within a year, Tammy &

I and our 2-year-old son launched into a faith ministry of music evangelism, moved to Texas, and traveled across the country and the world. We had no clue what we were doing! We just knew God had set this up, and we said "Yes" and went.

Big faith or young ignorant courage, you might think. But not really. It was simple obedience. The Lord drew such a picture for us and asked, "Will you?" It has been that way ever since. Then, about five years in, He gave us our daughter, Brooke, making our quartet complete.

After we had been on the road a couple of years, Tammy felt a prompting to have a marriage retreat with our Board of Directors; most of them were pastors involved at what was then *Lifeway's Fall Festivals of Marriage*. So, we held our first retreat at the Plains Baptist Assembly in Floydada, Texas.

These marriage celebrations became something we did just for fun, in between our music dates. We slowly organized things as time passed and based the ministry on Ecclesiastes 4:12, which says, "A cord of three strands is not easily broken." That had been our theme since our wedding day. We got married on August "31." I wrote a song for our wedding called *This Time*, which spoke of the three of us as One. So we took all of the above, and thus, Three2One Marriage Conferences were born.

Well, we had no idea what the state of marriage would be in our little world come 2023. It's somewhat unrecognizable. We have watched traditional, Biblical, man & wife relationships lose their sacred place in society. Many believe it's old-fashioned and being married isn't really necessary today. Somebody forgot that this was Jehovah God the Creator's idea, not ours! It's how every nation on the globe began—built on man, woman, and child—a FAMILY UNIT.

So, along with my wife and our God-picked Board of Directors, I would like to freely, yet vulnerably, share our stories with you. They are miracles. They are painful. They are beautiful. They are real because we are real everyday husbands & wives.

This book is designed to be used as a couple's weekly devotional. Once a week, for a year. Then yes, repeat! There are 52 devotions (including two "millennial" bonuses) that are meant to be read together at least every seven days.

These devotions will help you "Touch Base." And just like that favorite American ballgame, you must touch *every* base to make it home. We know how difficult it is to make/take time to connect, but our prayer is that this book will help.

We hope you know your marriage union is the most significant relationship you will have with another human being while breathing on this planet. **Your marriage will ultimately be your greatest achievement.** Not your career, talent, barns you built, or all you did for other people.

It is the picture of Jesus, the Groom, and Us, His Bride, united as One. When you've done it all, and it's back to just the two of you again, you will be blessed to know that person who's still sharing your bed after all those years. That's God's way. It's beautiful!

THE BENEFIT OF THE DOUBT

GIVE IT. And give it every day. Ladies, your husband loves you. He chose you. He married you. You're "the one" above all others. He's your husband.

And vice versa for the men. Your wife loves and respects you and wants what is best for you. Really. These are absolute truths. So, remind yourself of them—often!

The co-writers of this book's Foreword, Dr. Jimmy & Carol Ann Draper, have become sweet friends over the last few years. We have worked with them in church ministry and have hosted them as guest speakers for our annual Three2One Valentine's Conference on Lake Granbury. What a national treasure they are, and how humbling it is for us even to be known by them.

One of my favorite marriage tips is from Carol Ann, who shares how she & Jimmy have learned to head off a conflict before it becomes a fight. Okay, maybe you don't like the word "fight." I don't either! So let's call it an argument, heated disagreement, feud, quarrel, fracas, or flat rubbing each other the wrong way. This tip is for everyday husband & wife conflict prevention.

It probably will not work when you intentionally lash out to damage in battle mode. But when Jimmy says something (sorry, but generally it's the male) that Carol may have heard as hurtful, she will think *Jimmy has said something that requires me to remind myself that I'm his bride, lover, and queen. I'll choose to give him the benefit of the doubt.*

Then she tells him, "Jimmy, um, can you say what you just said in a *different* way?"

That gives him the chance to rethink, *Hmmm. Was it what I said or how I said it?* And that little technique can be magic!

Husbands can, at random times, speak to their wives in ways that sound offensive or hurtful and do not even realize it. We weren't trying to hurt her. It was our clear body language & our tone, TONE, **TONE**, TONE!

So, the next time one of you says "Whatever" to the other, and it hits you harder than it should, try this:

1. **Give the benefit of the doubt.** Remind yourself of those absolute truths that I mentioned at the start. Choose *not* to be easily offended. Then,
2. **Ask your spouse if they can say that in a *different* way.**

It may not be magic, but it can *literally* make some things disappear!

Love is not easily provoked or offended.
So, it is unloving to be easily offended.
1 Corinthians 13:5

—SHERMAN ATEN

Food for Thought

Review the phrases commonly used in marriage below. Practice saying them in a *different* way. Think about the tone that you might use to speak to them.

Will a gentler tone make a difference, as well?

- What's wrong? Nothing!
- You never do _____.
- You always do _____.
- You're just like your mother/father.
- Why do you take things so personally?

Do you see how these statements might be re-phrased in a way that gently but effectively keeps the lines of communication open? Determine that you will pause before saying something that could erode positive communication between you and your spouse.

THE BONES

MAYBE SOME of you have heard that song by Maren Morris called *The Bones*. If not, perhaps pause quickly and listen to give you more insight into what I will say. When my husband, Marshall, and I heard this song when it first came out in 2019, we were overwhelmed by how much we related to the lyrics when it came to our relationship. Like every couple, we have our ups, and we definitely have our downs. Here is some of our story.

Marshall and I grew up in the same hometown. We even attended the same church growing up. We knew "of" each other simply because he and my brother were friends. Since he was five years older than me, we never saw much of each other until later in life. It wasn't until after I graduated college that our paths crossed again. Then, a few times turned into more, and finally, we ended up dating. He became my best friend.

> **We leaned a lot on each other rather than God . . .**

We were together for three years before we got married. Although we were Christians and had a relationship with the Lord, our relationship wasn't perfect by any means. We leaned a lot on each other rather than God at the time and ended up living together before we got married.

Maybe you can relate to our story. Because of our relationship with the Lord, I struggled a lot with the conviction of us living together. I fought my conviction, thinking it was fine and we were okay. In today's culture, everyone lives together, right?

Deep down, I knew my relationship with the Lord was struggling, so Marshall moved out. We lived apart for one and a half years before we got married. And because of our obedience, we are now stronger than ever before.

We are grateful that our God is forgiving and full of redemption. Like the Psalms teach:

For You, Lord are good, and ready to forgive, and
abundant in loving kindness
to all who call upon you.
Psalm 86:5 NASB

As the song lyrics say, "When the bones are good, the rest don't matter. Yeah, the paint could peel, the glass could shatter. Let it break cause you and I remain the same." Because Marshall and I both had a relationship with Jesus, the Lord never gave up on us. Was it easy? No. It was challenging, and yes, the glass seemed to shatter a few times, but our relationship with the Lord only strengthened.

Surely goodness and mercy shall follow me all the
days of my life, and I will dwell
in the house of the Lord forever.
Psalm 23:6 NKJV

Good bones are the foundation of both of us having a personal relationship with Jesus and putting God first. Maybe you are or have been in a similar situation. Put God at the forefront of your relationship and see what He will do.

-BROOKE ATEN COCHRUM

Food for Thought

Sometimes, we justify sin with the excuse, "Everybody's doing it." But God doesn't excuse sin. And He doesn't honor our excuses. He forgives our repentant heart.

One of the oldest defenses around, since the days of Adam and Eve, is to blame another for *our* sins. If you're old enough, you remember a television comedian whose tagline was, "The devil made me do it." The devil cannot force you to do anything, including disobeying God's laws. He will, however, try to influence your viewpoint so you fall into the trap of justification for sinful actions.

Read the following scripture passages. What excuses did each person make, and what should they have done instead? How can we learn from them?

- Luke 14:16-24, the guests at the king's banquet

- John 5:1-15, the man at the pool of Bethesda

- Exodus 32:22-24, Aaron, the brother of Moses

- Judges 6:12-15, Gideon

- Genesis 3:12, Adam and Genesis 3:13, Eve

THE DANCE

I GREW UP in West Texas. So Country and Western tracks indent my mental wiring that is tuned to masculine messages in C&W mashups:

- ✓ **Work Hard** – Preferably on a dirt road with a farm.
- ✓ **Drink Harder** – Ain't Nothing a Beer Can't Fix, Ain't no Pain it can't wash away.
- ✓ **Hook up** – Just Knocking Boots, Had to Have You.
- ✓ **Worship Conveniently** – That's What I Love About Sunday mornings.

Confusion arises as we select tracks and false melodies with mistaken lyrics about what it means to be male. Most notes that are played come from the wrong jukeboxes.

Growing up, I learned three ditties:

- ✓ Big Boys don't cry.
- ✓ Boys will be boys. *And,*
- ✓ Boys win at all costs.

Can we download a melody to escape tunnel vision, blind spots, and sideways energy to mold boys into men and men into better men? The Bible sings a broader story of a bigger life with a better future. With apologies to Maren Morris, Jesus provides good bones. Hence, the foundation is solid even if the paint peels and the glass shatters.

Genesis 1:27 views men and women as kings and queens, created to co-rule with two aces in the hole: Dignity and diversity. Men are designed to carefully wield authority, own responsibility, provide security, and live productively.

But shared regency is not wearing crowns, drinking out of goblets, and shouting Dilly-Dilly. Co-regency is a helpful metaphor for our co-rule with God as kings. If men dance to the music downloaded by our Creator, they will care for what's entrusted to them (jobs, wives, kids) like God Himself. People can get a clearer picture of the dance God designs by watching godly men reflect His goodness and grace as we live out loud.

Here's the reality. I'm not a good dancer. I'm Baptist. I stumble and tumble and somehow can't combine the melody and the rhythm. Most of us, in a similar way, aren't fluid in faith and miss the music God plays. Our hearts are tuned to appealing ear candy that leads us the wrong way. We know the proper chorus in our gut, but we dance to silly little jingles and singles crafted by false composers that create catchy tunes that curse our culture.

How can wives help? Cheer your husband on when he leads. Compliment his awkward attempts to live the dance of Jesus. Go out of your way to compliment the smallest step in His dance. You'll find him dancing more and loving better.

—DR. JOE STEWART

Food for Thought

It's time to play some good music and dance the night away with your spouse. Choose one of the following ideas to find a deeper connection:

- Write a note telling your mate, expressing love and appreciation for how they care for everything God has given them.
- Allow your partner to lead a dance or two. Take a moment's break from "decision-making" and let them choose a restaurant or instruct the kids without your input.
- Work to find synchrony in the rhythm of your week. If your partner sleeps late, keep the house quiet. If they stay up late, extend your day briefly to find balance and understanding in your relationship.

DEBITS AND DEPOSITS

AS OUR FATHER IS, so should we be. Obviously, He is all things that we can't be without Him. And He wouldn't even ask us to be like Him if He didn't give us every resource needed to empower us to be so (i.e., The Holy Spirit). But according to Luke 24:49, that power surfaces only if we really want it.

Let's take your bank account first. This, right here, has been known to blow a marriage out of the water for good. Money has been the grounds for divorce, so often, it switches places with infidelity as Numero Uno at the top of the "Reasons for Divorce" chart.

So, how is it that we should be like Him when it comes to the amount of dollars we make? Well, know this: He is a Giver. Really! He is The Ultimate Giver.

And just like that, we are made and meant to give. But "hello." Our nature is bent in the opposite direction. You may not want to admit that, but it is our selfish flesh that we must deal with daily. You may like to give and even put others and their needs ahead of yours. But at some point, when it's just you sitting alone in your chair at night, you may think you haven't gotten what you deserve from someone—your kids, spouse, friends, or church. Eeeewww, there it is. But let's get back on track . . . *money.*

I have a friend who came to Christ later in life. But when He did, he made a complete 'bout-face' in his thoughts and behavior.

And that's what repentance looks like. One thing that happened with his finances is one of the most inspiring and convicting things I know about him.

He began trying to do things God's way, even using Dave Ramsey's Financial Peace to kickstart things (which is a good idea for most of us). My friend told me when he writes down his budget, which he regularly does, he puts all his tithes, offerings, gifts to others, and things that his left hand doesn't know about in the "plus +" column.

They are not listed in the debits. Spiritually, that is so correct! Where your treasure is, there will your heart be. The work must start with your motives; your giving will always be a heart issue.

Let's take marriage, for instance. Our Father is the original author of this "love life" we have with our husband or wife. As sinful creatures, we will fail over the journey—debiting our account. And we will do that a lot over the years.

The work must start with your motives; your giving will always be a heart issue.

But just as in your *literal* bank account, you can only debit if you have enough deposits. Oh, you can make some debits without enough deposits to cover them. But then you'd better look out because overdraft charges, returned checks, embarrassing letters & phone calls will put you in the Red Zone! And once the damage is done, it won't soon be forgotten by your bank or the person/business who got the shaft.

And in your marriage account, those overdrafts won't be totally forgotten, either. Love indeed covers a multitude. But that means you have made enough deposits to cover these, sometimes mindless, debits you've taken the past month or over the last 30 minutes. You have also intentionally made several deposits during that time, so you're operating in the black with no red number overages.

I am not saying you need to keep your balance near zero. The number of debits must always be *less* than the number of deposits. If you have a recurring debit from your account every week, you will probably start paying fees for that to be processed automatically. That's a fee you *could* & *should* avoid!

—SHERMAN ATEN

Food for Thought

Consider these questions as you assess the debits and deposits within your marriage.

- Have we been making financial decisions as a team?
- Are we giving as the Lord would lead us to do, with a cheerful attitude?
- Have we made enough deposits into our marriage to take a debit when it hits the marriage bank? Check the balance on your spouse's account; they will tell you.

Make a determined effort to increase the "value" in your marital bank account. Ask the Lord to change your heart into that of a giver—physically and spiritually.

DEFINING MOMENTS— CHOOSE WISELY

SOME OF YOU might remember the old Indiana Jones movies with Harrison Ford. In one of them, they search for the Holy Grail—the cup Jesus drank out of at the Last Supper. So, in the movie, Indiana Jones finds the Grail, but the bad guys (the Germans) are also there and are determined to have the cup for themselves.

Now, in the room are many cups, and the true Grail is among them. The Knight guarding the Grail tells the bad guys to "choose wisely." The bad guy chooses the gold cup because it is a cup for a King. Let's just say he dies rather quickly, and the Knight says, "he chose poorly."

Then, it's Indiana Jones's turn to choose. He looks among the cups and picks a very ordinary cup, as if it were a carpenter's cup. He drinks, and the Knight says, "You chose wisely."

In life, there are many "defining moments." Those times when there are choices to be made that can affect or alter one's path. These can happen to us individually, in our marriages, and in our families.

When our oldest daughter Jennifer was getting married to Tyler, at their rehearsal dinner, I told the story of what I saw as a defining moment in Jennifer's life. When she was a little girl, probably about five, she and I went to our land to fly a kite. We had cleared the ground but hadn't started building anything yet. Some barbed wire was strung across the gate area with a ribbon on it.

As I was getting the stuff out of my jeep, Jennifer bolted toward the gate area, as she couldn't wait to fly her kite. I yelled, "Jennifer! No!" But it was too late; she hit that barbed wire strung across the opening, and she got "clotheslined," hitting right in the neck area. It was a brutal hit, flipping her off her feet.

I ran over and picked her up, holding her ever so tightly. After she stopped crying, I checked her all over, and she appeared to be okay. I said, "Jen, why don't we just go home? We can fly your kite another day."

She said, "No, Daddy. I want to stay and fly my kite."

She wiped away her tears, and we had a marvelous time flying her kite. I believe that was a defining moment in Jen's life. It spoke to me about my daughter and showed me she wasn't a quitter; she persevered.

This attitude served her well during challenging times, such as when her mom and I divorced for three years. That was the result of many poor choices of mine. And, when her sister Alyssa passed. It would have been easy for Jennifer to curl up and feel sorry for herself, thinking *Why me?* But she didn't— she chose to live and trust God. Well-known American minister and author Henry Blackaby refers to these times as a "crisis of belief that requires faith and action."

We are living in defining moment times.

Currently, we are living in defining moment times. We face choices daily; some take us down the easy path of death even though the enemy calls it a path of life. Then, there is the more difficult way, the actual path of life that Jesus points us to.

In the Old Testament, Joshua was a great military leader, essentially second in command after Moses. He helped lead the Israelites into the Promised Land after Moses died. And times were just as difficult back in Joshua's day; people had to make wise choices. Here's what Joshua had to say:

> ***Choose for yourselves*** *this day whom you will serve, whether the gods which your fathers served that were on the other side of the River, or the gods of the Amorites, in whose land you dwell. But as for me and my house, we will serve the Lord.*
> Joshua 24:15 NKJV [Emphasis added]

Joshua chose wisely. Will you?

—SCOTT DIX

Food for Thought

Reflect on your choices this week concerning your spouse and children. Which were wise, and which would you like to have back? Discuss with your spouse, admit your mistakes, and ask for forgiveness if necessary.

Think back over your life and reflect upon those "defining moments." Consider the effect they have had on you or *still* affect you to this day. Ask God to show His perspective on those moments and respond to what He shows you.

Finally, consider the choices you need to make from now on that will intentionally move you, your marriage, and your family closer to the Lord. Write them down and make them a matter of prayer.

Father, thank you for loving us and caring about every detail of our lives. Thank you for always dealing with us in truth and leading us down the path of life. Please guide us with your Spirit to make wise choices that will strengthen our family and marriage. May our choices glorify you, Lord Jesus, and bring honor to your name. Amen.

DINNER WITH A PROFILE

CLOSE YOUR EYES and think about one of the best dinners you have ever experienced. Maybe it was a romantic night with your spouse or a special occasion, like an anniversary or a birthday. We eat many dinners throughout life, but a few special ones stand above the rest—forever etched in our memory.

I can still recall that night on our honeymoon with Lori in 1987 when we went on a dinner cruise off the island of Maui. It was so awesome! Little did we know we would be divorced eight years and three kids later. However, after three more years, the Lord did a miracle by saving me and restoring our marriage and family.

Once back together, I poured myself into reading God's word. One day, I read Ephesians 5:25, where husbands are commanded to love their wives "just as Christ loved the church and gave himself up" for her. After reading that, I remember asking, "Lord, how do I do that?" That is such a tall order, then I sincerely prayed, "Lord, please teach me how to do that practically and daily."

A while later, we attended a small marriage conference of six couples in Fort Worth led by Sherman & Tammy Aten. The conference would begin on Friday evening with a "date night" and run through Saturday afternoon. They took us to an Outback Steakhouse (good start). There, they handed us each a "Love

Language Profile" from the book *The Five Love Languages* by Dr. Gary Chapman (a must-read book).

We were asked to fill out the profile individually during dinner and discuss the results with our spouses afterward. Oh, my goodness! While sharing our profile results, Lori and I nearly fell out of our chairs.

It was like God shined a spotlight from heaven on the profiles at our table, clearly showing us where we had failed in our marriage and how to correct it. I will never forget that moment for as long as I live! Let me explain.

You see, in Gary's book, he describes a visual of a "love tank" inside every person. When we feel loved, our love tank is full; when we don't, our love tank is running on empty. He then describes how there are five ways that people speak and understand emotional love, which he calls "The Five Love Languages." Jesus is the Master of each, and they are:

- ✓ Words of Affirmation
- ✓ Quality Time
- ✓ Acts of Service
- ✓ Physical Touch
- ✓ Gifts

We like all these love languages. However, one will "fill up" our personal love tank more quickly, which is our primary love language. And if neglected, we will most often complain.

In addition, since we feel most loved when receiving our primary love language, we tend to express love to our spouse in that same manner. The problem is husbands and wives typically don't speak the same language. Rarely does a husband have the same primary love language as his wife. And vice versa.

For example, my primary love language is Physical Touch (I'm a hugger), with Words of Affirmation a close second. However, Lori's primary love language is Quality Time, with Words of Affirmation as her second.

I reacted to not having enough physical touch (sexual and non-sexual) by complaining and criticizing Lori. I would withdraw and not spend time with her, even talking down to her, which drained her love tank.

She responded in a like manner with even less physical touch and complaining and criticizing me. We were both drained as we continually had the same fights with the same results. And which eventually ended with our divorce.

But now, armed with the knowledge of what truly made each other feel most loved, we need only to practice it, which we did! I wrote Lori's love language and personality type, as well as our girls, on a post-it note. I keep it in my wallet as a reminder to always love them in the way they feel most loved. The apostle Peter instructs:

Husbands, likewise, dwell with your wives
with understanding.
1 Peter 3:7 NKJV

To paraphrase, I need to know my wife's strengths, weaknesses, likes, dislikes, personality, and how she feels most loved. Our marriage flourished when I began to study Lori; I'm still studying! Our relationship continues to get better and better as I love her unselfishly, the way God created her. And I try not to change her to what *I* think she should be for me.

Since then, the Lord has continued to grow us in many ways as he continues to teach us. We even became involved in the Marriage Ministry with Sherman and Tammy, helping others avoid the painful mistakes we made early on. We can offer couples practical advice for a godly relationship.

But it all began with a simple prayer: "Lord, teach me." And God answered that prayer through a dinner with a profile.

—Scott & Lori Dix

Food for Thought

How well do you know what makes your spouse feel most loved (i.e., their love language)? Do you know their strengths, weaknesses, their personality type, etc.? Have you taken the time to study them?

What has your spouse or children complained about to you? For example, "Honey, it seems like you are always working; you don't spend any time with us," or "Dad, you never buy me anything," or "I don't like when you say that to me." These may be a clue as to their primary love language. Read the book *The Five Love Languages* by Dr. Gary Chapman. It will help you better understand yourself, your spouse, your children, and even your work relationships.

Consider areas in your marriage and family where you desire improvement. Have you prayed about them? Take an honest look in the mirror. What do you need to ask God to teach you about? Better yet, ask Him for his perspective—maybe you'll get a dinner with a profile!

Father, thank you for your Word and the wonderful gift of marriage and family. Please show me and teach me practical ways to love my spouse and children better and understand them more intimately. Please help me respond in obedience to what you reveal. In Jesus' name. Amen.

D.I.V.O.R.C.E.

ACCORDING TO STATISTICS, half of the readers of this devotion will go through or have gone through a divorce. Since I haven't experienced divorce, I won't pretend to understand all the emotions involved. But I can acknowledge the words and actions sometimes said and done in the name of "love." Words offered in the name of Christ but received as anything but loving or Christlike—even when unintentionally spoken.

Growing up in a Christian denomination, I believed divorce and Christian leadership were mutually exclusive. Somehow, a fallen marriage meant a fallen person. And as I grew older, I continued to believe that was true.

But I also realized how many other ways there are to fall. In fact, I learned that *all* of us have fallen. And instead of steamrolling downhill, the Cross made the ground level for everyone. The only reason some folks didn't get back up was that they were being held down.

It's not about the deficiencies of a particular practice—whatever it is. It is about how God loves us, even when others struggle. It's not about what is being done wrong but about doing what is right. It's not about a person falling but about helping someone up. And it's not about hurting, but healing.

Marriage is a godly concept. Divorce is worldly. And the Bible makes it plain that God's children are not *of* the world, although we are certainly *in* it. Not everything goes according to plan, but nothing is beyond God's grace.

Things happen. Some marriages end in divorce. This is not a news flash. And because the dissolution of a marriage is often public and raw, the people involved and who need to sense God's love the most often feel it the least. Shame on us!

A troubled marriage is not a reason to give up. There is no escaping God's forgiveness; with both partners humbly letting God lead, healing can occur. Forgiveness involves accepting the Truth, assigning it an appropriate value, and putting it on your private altar before God.

> *A troubled marriage is not a reason to give up . . . healing can occur.*

A strong marriage is a reason to give thanks. It is to be appreciated and protected. It is to be loved and prayed for. Those who have had marriages dissolved are not to be pitied and certainly not judged. They are to be treated like everyone else who falls and must get back up. And they are to be loved and prayed for.

—KIM LANIER

Food for Thought

Divorce doesn't fix that which is broken. It is not nearly as effective as working with the Lord to heal the hurts that have caused a marriage to become troubled. Consider these thoughts to avoid the painful sting resulting from the possible or eminent dissolution of a marriage:

- Avoid playing the victim. Guilt is not from God, and placing blame or shame on the other partner is not a Christ-like behavior.
- View your anger, resentment, and hurt through the lens of Christ. Men despised and rejected him. Yet He took on the iniquity of us all.
- Learn from your mistakes. Allow the Lord to point out repetitive behaviors that cause you to fall.
- When you feel negativity rising toward your spouse (or ex-spouse), replace the thoughts with something positive. Research shows that it takes five positive thoughts to change the direction of one negative. Move in the right direction by controlling your thoughts.

ENJOY MOMENTS

MARSHALL AND I were married on January 10, 2020, or 1.10.20 (*Yes, we 100% planned that!*). We will never forget the love and generosity poured into that special day. During our ceremony, one of my bridesmaids approached me at just the right moment and said these words in my ear, "Don't forget to stop and take it all in."

Wow, I thought. That was such a good reminder.

How many of us need to remember to stop and take it all in? Especially in our marriages. It's kind of like when you take a picture to capture a special moment. Life can be busy, and things can feel scattered. But it is in those moments, when we allow our minds to embrace all His goodness, we can see the beautiful blessings the Lord has given us.

Be still and know that I am God.
Psalm 46:10 NIV

Because of Jesus, we have victory in the Lord and confidence in eternal life in Him. There is no greater love or gift.

Marshall and I now have a daughter named Kinna Blair, who brings us so much joy and laughter. After having a child, enjoying moments has become much clearer to both of us. People have advised, "Enjoy this time. Pay attention. She won't be this young for much longer."

Marriage is a gift, a true blessing from God. There is so much reward in our marriage relationship when Marshall and I take the time to enjoy moments together. To truly enjoy them.

Don't forget to experience special moments with your spouse. Continue to date, even after the children come along. Check on your spouse throughout the day. Pay attention to their needs and desires. Take the time to listen rather than respond. These actions are essential to the health and well-being of your marriage.

—BROOKE ATEN COCHRUM

Food for Thought

Moments come in two varieties: ordinary and *extra*-ordinary. In marriage, daily routines can make everything seem ordinary or mundane. And the reality is that moments can be fleeting if we don't capture them.

Make a list of creative ways to turn ordinary moments into memorable ones, using the ideas below as a starting point:

- Schedule regular date nights. Plan them out for several weeks in advance, giving you each something to look forward to.
- Take a class together.
- Go bowling or attend a sports event (for a local or a pro team).
- Visit a local museum.
- Take a long walk, holding hands all along the way.
- Make some popcorn and watch a movie together.
- Look through a photo album while snuggling on the couch.
- Go fly a kite (literally!).
- Eat breakfast for dinner.

Add your ideas to the list:

_____

_____

_____

_____

_____

FINDING COMPLETENESS IN CHRIST

SOMETIMES WE HEAR people, including engaged couples, speak of looking forward to being married because they say that will make them "complete" as a person. While a husband and wife joining together can be very beneficial in complementing each other's strengths and compensating for each other's weaknesses, your worth or identity is not wrapped up in anyone other than the person of Jesus Christ. Getting married will not instantly satisfy you if you are not content or fulfilled before marriage.

Many people yearn for specific situations to develop before they think they will feel complete. Even if you achieve certain goals like marriage, kids, or career success, they won't bring long-term satisfaction. If you are not complete as an individual, marriage will not complete you. Parenthood will not complete you. Success will not complete you. As wonderful as those things can be, your completeness does not depend on anyone or anything else.

Colossians 2:10 says, "You have been given fullness in Christ." Before working on any self-improvement program or looking to anyone or anything else for affirmation, recognize that you are precious to God just the way you are, created in His image, and dearly loved by Him with an everlasting love (Jeremiah 31:3).

SHERMAN & TAMMY ATEN

Completeness is not found in circumstances as individuals or as a couple. In our marriage, we dealt with infertility for five years. We encountered other couples struggling with the issue of infertility who merely existed in their marriage, waiting for their circumstances to change.

A couple is a family, whether you have children or not. If you have a child who passes away, as heartbreaking as that grief is, you do not cease to be a family. You are still a family once your children grow up and you become empty nesters. The stress of challenging situations can drive a couple apart, or they can choose to find unity as they come on their knees together before our Heavenly Father.

The apostle Paul wrote that he had learned to be content in all circumstances (Philippians 4:11). It wasn't that Paul's circumstances were always pleasant. He had experienced intense persecution, unjust treatment, and great hardships (and remember, Paul did not have a helpmate wife to assist him). Paul realized his completeness was found in his identity in Christ Jesus, not in circumstances, others, or success. As unworthy as he knew he was, Paul had the assurance that God's grace made him who he was (1 Corinthians 15:10).

Allow God's grace to shape you.

Allow God's grace to shape you so that you might find completeness in being adopted as one of God's children in Christ Jesus. Remember also, your marriage was made complete when you became husband and wife.

—ED & ELIZABETH PLANTS

Food for Thought

Being complete in Christ means having a sense of wholeness and fulfillment through a personal relationship with Jesus. We find our purpose and identity through new life in Him.

Yet even after becoming a new creation in Christ, we still live out the role of a husband/wife, father/mother, or son/daughter. How do we no longer look to other sources for our validation, particularly within the bonds of marriage?

Just as in the relationship between Christ and His church, as a couple, you are part of the larger "whole." Your completeness includes Him, who holds everything together. Consider these questions as you embrace the notion that marriage goes beyond an earthly bond.

- Are there times you feel less than complete?
- What are some ways your spouse can help you remember you are special to God just the way you are?
- When difficulties arise, what can we do as a couple to grow closer to each other and closer to God instead of growing apart?

FORGIVENESS

I WAS SITTING in church alone because the girls were with their dad for the weekend. The guest preacher started talking about forgiveness and how we must *give* it to *receive* it. *Wow!* I thought. My bitterness and hardness towards my ex-husband had blinded me to all God had for me.

In that moment, God opened my mind and heart to fully understand that I won't be forgiven if I cannot forgive. *Oh my.* And when I said, "I forgive Scott," God flooded my soul with unbelievable peace and acceptance of my circumstances. At that moment, I thought, *I want the best for him.* And with that came an understanding of my own faults and failures as a wife and mother. It was the moment that changed my life and future.

When I let go of the hurt, it was amazing how God filled my heart with love—His love. With His love came an understanding of our sinfulness. And the knowledge of my sin showed me that I had no place to judge anyone; that is God's place only.

People ask me how I could forgive so completely everything that happened. I always tell them it wasn't me but God that did it. He is the only trustworthy source of peace, love, and forgiveness. And in standing before a holy and righteous God, we realize that we are all sinners, which puts us all on the same level playing field.

Understanding our own sins and what Jesus did for us on the Cross frees us to be forgiving people as we were forgiven.

Ephesians 4:32 teaches us to "Be kind and compassionate to one another, forgiving each other, just as in Christ God forgave you."

There is much truth in the saying:

> **A happy marriage is the union of two good forgivers.**

—SCOTT & LORI DIX

Food for Thought

As you consider this teaching on forgiveness, grab your Bible. Then, openly and honestly answer the following questions:

- According to Matthew 6:14-15, who in your life needs your forgiveness?
- Do you truly understand your sinfulness? Reference 1 John 3:4, Exodus 20:1-17, Matthew 5:17-48.
- Do you find yourself judging people harshly and applying different standards to them than you apply to yourself? Reference Matthew 7:1-5, John 7:24.

Father, please help me to forgive others as I have been forgiven. Jesus, thank you for going to the Cross for me. Help me to be honest with you about my sin, confessing and turning from it. I leave the judging up to you as you are the true Judge. May our marriage truly be a union of two good forgivers. In Jesus' name. Amen.

THE GOD OF ALL COMFORT

SOMETIMES, people have the mistaken idea that the Christian life is supposed to be easy or that God has promised a trouble-free life if we follow Him. On the contrary, Jesus promised, "In this world, you will have trouble." But He also went on to say, "I have told you these things, so that in me you may have peace" (John 16:33).

Not everything we experience in life will be without difficulties. Yet God will still be present, and He will still be working.

After being married for five years, we began actively trying to have children. The next five years of experiencing infertility were a roller coaster of getting our hopes up and then having those hopes crushed again, month after month. As hard as those years were, looking back, we see blessings that God was giving us even in those circumstances. We got to travel more, participate in ministry together, and experience things that otherwise would not have happened. Another blessing was the people God brought into our lives to comfort and pray with us during those discouraging days of infertility.

A recurrent pattern began to emerge when we experienced challenges in our lives. These included the pain of infertility, the unknowns of adopting, the added dimensions of adopting a bi-racial child, eventually giving birth to five more children, and parenting six kids within an eleven-year span. Additionally, our dads both died before we had children, which meant our children would not get to know their wonderful grandpas. Also, we went through the incredible stress of Ed being forced out of a job.

The pattern we saw emerge in these situations was that God comforted us and blessed us with people who helped us through each circumstance. The promise the Lord gave to Isaiah was lived out for us:

> *When you pass through the waters, I will be with*
> *you; and when you pass through the rivers,*
> *they will not sweep over you.*
> *When you walk through the fire,*
> *you will not be burned, the flames will not set you*
> *ablaze. For I am the Lord, your God,*
> *the Holy One of Israel, your Savior.*
> Isaiah 43:2-3a NIV

But we also saw something else happen. Once we emerged on the other side of these experiences, God would bring people into our lives who were going through the same struggles and needed to hear a word of hope. One of our life verses became:

> *Praise be to the God and Father of our Lord Jesus*
> *Christ, the Father of compassion and the God of all*
> *comfort, who comforts us in all our troubles so that*
> *we can comfort those in any trouble with the*
> *comfort we ourselves have received from God.*
> 2 Corinthians 1:3-4 NIV

When you are experiencing difficulties, look to God for help and hope, and then be ready to minister to others with the same compassion and comfort you receive.

—ED & ELIZABETH PLANTS

Food for Thought

The Lord uses people within the body of Christ to bring compassion and comfort to others in their time of need. Take time, as a couple, to reflect on the questions below.

Allow yourself to be mindful of the blessings of God that have come through the storms of life. Praise Him for walking with you and providing the ministry of others.

- Can we name people who have blessed us during challenging times?
- How have we experienced God's presence during times of struggle that we did not recognize during good times?
- During tranquil times, how might we as a couple prepare for possible future difficulties?
- Who are the people who need us to pay forward the blessings of encouragement and comfort in this moment?

GOD SHOW ME

LOOKING BACK at our first marriage was painful. Fights were never reconciled—we fought repeatedly. If you're in that relationship, you may ask, "Can God really give us the marriage that dreams are made of?"

The answer is unequivocally "YES!" because the Bible teaches:

> *You will find him if you seek him*
> *with all your heart and all your soul.*
> Deuteronomy 4:29 NKJV

When God put us back together, we knew we had to seek **Him** to experience a good, healthy, loving marriage. So, first, He put wonderful mentors into our lives to show us how to love each other. God revealed where we went wrong through their example by studying the scriptures and reading wonderful books like *Love Languages* by Gary Chapman and *Love & Respect* by Dr. Emerson Eggerichs.

The Lord showed us how self-focused we were. And to have a strong marriage, we must become "other-focused," putting the needs of our spouse above our own. In addition, he showed us that we needed to learn not to be offended by every little thing. We must choose not to be offended and choose to love every day.

A man's wisdom gives him patience;
it is to his glory to overlook an offense.
Proverbs 19:11 NIV

Now, being *re*-married for 22 years, it gets better every day. We understand that having God at the center is the key to a loving marriage. This doesn't mean that every day is easy; we have endured many hard times and trying times. But we made a covenant before God, and he has blessed us with amazing lives to bring him glory.

—SCOTT & LORI DIX

Food for Thought

It is a scientific fact that what one focuses on will direct the steps of one's life (and marriage). As humans, we have a large capacity to focus on many things. So, we often cast our view on unimportant things that won't make a difference.

Reflect on the questions below to help redirect your attention toward the priorities in your life.

- Do you look to your spouse for happiness or to God?
- Are you easily offended? Did you realize you can choose not to be? Reference Proverbs 19:11, 12:16.
- Make a list of choices you made today towards your spouse. Would you describe your choices as "proactive" or "reactive?"
- What would God want to change in you and your marriage from now on? Reference James 1:19-25.

Father, please help me to put you first in my life. Please show me areas of selfishness in my life and marriage. Help me choose wisely, not being easily offended, but giving grace, walking the path of love, being a doer of your word and not a hearer only. We pray in Jesus' name. Amen.

HOW DOES YOUR BOOK READ?

MY FATHER WAS a Pulitzer Prize-winning writer and author. He used to tell me the most challenging part of writing anything was the beginning and the end. The beginning and the end are basically a summary of the middle. So, you must know your middle well before introducing the beginning! And the end? Well, sometimes the end hasn't yet arrived.

Have you ever read a book that you couldn't put down? One where each page demanded that you read the next and then the next. Sometimes, the suspense creates a bit of anxiety as to what the ending will be. You find yourself thinking, *Will my favorite character live or die? Will the conflict end happily?*

Often, we are tempted to sneak a peak at the last chapter when reading a book. After all, this might allow us to relax and enjoy the unfinished chapters. Knowing the ending may make you feel you can endure whatever you read. But that's not how life works!

Our lives are chapters. Some are joyous. And others come with surprises that knock our feet right out from under us. Divorce, sickness, finances, death, and wayward children take our joy away. We want so badly to know how we will make it to the next day. And like a book, we must proverbially keep reading, one page at a time, as we make our way to the end.

God is so good and merciful. He has already taught us about the end. You would think that since we know the end, we could relax

SHERMAN & TAMMY ATEN

and find peace in each day. However, even Christians who know where they will be at the end of the book still allow fear and anxiety to write their chapters.

Reflecting on my life, I understand that during my darkest moments, when it seemed like God was far away, He was actually the closest—comforting, leading, and carrying me. In those times, I would yell at Him that it was too much. I would beg for answers and plead for Him to "take it away."

But that's not how it worked. Each day, I was given new strength until the chapter was over. Then, I saw what He carried me through. And most importantly, my relationship with Him became closer and more intimate.

Each chapter prepared me for the next, with total reliance on Him. What does your story look like? Mine is a love story. Through those dark times, He wrote an incredible love story.

And the end of the story? Well, it's already written. And yes, I did sneak a peek at the end of The Book. And for the whole world, it is the greatest love story ever told.

— ALICE GILROY

For God so loved the world that He gave His one and only Son, that whoever believes in Him, should not perish but have everlasting life.
John 3:16 NIV

Very truly I tell you, whoever hears my word and believes him who sent me has eternal life and will not be judged but has crossed over from death to life. Very truly I tell you, a time is coming and has now come when the dead will hear the voice of the

*Son of God and those who hear will live. For as the
Father has life in himself, so he has granted the Son
also to have life in himself. And he has given him
authority to judge because he is the Son of Man.
Do not be amazed at this, for a time is coming when
all who are in their graves will hear his voice and
come out—those who have done what is good will
rise to live, and those who have done
what is evil will rise to be condemned.*

John: 5: 24-29 NIV

Food for Thought

The Bible teaches that we should always be ready to give the reason for our hope (1 Peter 3:15). In other words, we should be prepared to share our testimony. 2 Timothy 1:8 says, Do not be ashamed of the testimony of the Lord.

Your testimony is your story. Like a book, it has chapters that unfold with each season. But you won't know what happens if you never turn the page. Reflect on the thoughts below as you compare your life's story to a physical book.

- Books outlast their author. Psalm 145:4 says, "Tell of His mighty deeds from generation to generation." Have you considered that your life will have a lasting impact on others? What legacy do you hope to leave through the word of your testimony?
- Good stories have plot twists and turns that help keep a reader engaged. What twists or turns has your life taken that came unexpectedly but brought newfound strength and reliance on the Lord?
- Our testimonies encourage others in the faith. How are you encouraging others in their darkest moments, but the word of *your* testimony? Are there opportunities for you to support others who are afraid to turn to the page in their life?

HOW HEAVENLY-MINDED IS YOUR HOME?

PAUL WROTE some excellent advice for building a meaningful marriage and home.

> *Therefore, as God's chosen people, holy and dearly loved, clothe yourselves with compassion, kindness, humility, gentleness, and patience. Bear with each other and forgive whatever grievances you may have against one another. Forgive as the Lord forgave you. And over all these virtues put on love, which binds them all together in perfect unity.*
>
> Colossians 3:13-14 NIV

Obviously, Paul is talking to followers of Jesus, or "God's chosen people, holy and dearly loved." As we grow and mature as believers, certain things are expected of us. Characteristics such as compassion, kindness, humility, gentleness, and patience are to be increasingly evident in how we treat one another.

In this passage, "Bear with each other" reminds us that resolving conflicts and disagreements in a positive, healthy manner is critical in keeping love alive and strong.

Forgiving "whatever grievances you may have against one another" is absolutely essential to maintaining peaceful and bonding relationships. Paul makes it even more profound by saying, "Forgive as the Lord forgave you." Paul also wrote:

Accept one another, then,
just as Christ accepted you,
in order to bring praise to God.
Romans 15:7 NIV

The key to all these positive characteristics is love. As Paul encourages us, we must "put on love, which binds them all together in perfect unity."

Robert Quillen wrote:

The one word above all others that makes a marriage successful is "ours."

If a person is not loved and accepted at home, somewhere, someone will take them in—and you probably won't like the results! If we have love, acceptance, compassion, kindness, forgiveness, humility, gentleness, and patience in our homes, we can create a little piece of heaven on earth.

—GLENN WARD

Food for Thought

What makes a home "Heavenly-Minded?" It is one that practices heavenly habits. These habits are formed when each household member determines to set their mind on the things above and not on the things of this world (Colossians 3:1-4).

Because we don't yet live in heaven, we often treat it like something coming in our future rather than something to be lived in the present. Christ is in our *now*. And when we allow the world's cares to consume our minds, we miss the opportunity to reflect heaven on earth.

Establish heavenly habits by integrating some of the ideas below into your daily routine. Allow heaven to be part of your day-to-day living.

- Recite the Lord's prayer each morning. Invite the kingdom of God into the next 24 hours, asking Jesus to be ever-present throughout your schedule.
- Say a prayer of thanks before each meal, even when you're out in public. Remember that we share heaven with others when practicing Christ-minded habits.
- Forgive and pray for people who have negatively interrupted your day. Whether intentional or unintentional, their actions may have resulted from something deeper than what is seen on the surface.

I FIXED WHAT YOU BROKE

HAVE YOU EVER tried to fix something and soon realized it was beyond your knowledge, ability, or resources to repair it? That happens often to me with cars, mowers, or anything electrical. It can be even more frustrating if you are the one who broke it to begin with. This realization happened to me in my marriage.

My wife Lori and I were married in 1987; our marriage really struggled from the start as I was a very selfish individual. My expectations for marriage were twofold: sex, all the time, and dinner on the table when I got home. God was not a part of our lives, although we would have told you we believed in God. However, we had no relationship with him.

We had our oldest daughter, Jennifer, in 1990 and our middle daughter, Alyssa, in 1992. We grew farther apart with the additional stress of children in an already struggling marriage. About six months after Alyssa was born, I began to party all the time. I started an adulterous relationship with a woman at work who was already married to her third husband. She divorced him right away.

This adultery continued for a couple of years, and then Lori found out. At the time, Lori was six months pregnant with our youngest daughter, Brianna. We separated for good a month or so after Brianna was born and eventually divorced.

I moved in with this other woman and about a year later married her. I didn't care anymore and felt like a "walking dead"—wholly broken inside. That's when God began to surround me with strong Christians at work. One coworker was a man named Ron, who gave me a bible. I began to read why I was broken; it was due to my sin. I was a liar, a thief, and an adulterer; I needed to be "fixed." Jesus Christ took care of that in June of 1998 when I got down on my hands and knees and asked him to forgive me of my sins and to save my soul. The moment I did that, somehow, I knew I was fixed—completely changed on the inside.

*Therefore, if anyone is in Christ, he is a new
creation; old things have passed away;
behold all things have become new.*
2 Corinthians 5:17 NKJV

The amazing thing is God didn't stop there. After He saved me, I ended the adulterous relationship that should never have started. I then prayed to the Lord on a Thursday night that he would somehow restore my marriage and family that I had managed to destroy. I had no hope of that happening, as Lori and I had been divorced for three years. But three days after my prayer, Lori asked if she could speak to me, so we talked while sitting in my car.

She looked at me and asked for my forgiveness for her part in the breakup of our marriage. After I picked my mouth up off the floor, I told her I forgave her and asked her to forgive me. She said, "I already have!"

I then told her I had received Jesus Christ as my Lord and Savior and decided to end the adulterous relationship that should never have begun. At that very moment, it was as if God was in the vehicle with us, and we were the only two people on the face of the earth. His presence was overwhelming. He told me, "Here's your opportunity; here's the answer to your prayer. I fixed what you broke."

Knowing what God wanted me to do, I looked at Lori and told her what I had prayed only three days earlier, and she began sobbing. She then told me that she had dropped to her knees last night and prayed the very same prayer!

So, we went in and told our girls we were getting back together and would never separate again. Alyssa said, "Daddy, it's a miracle," and I agreed!

I told my daughter, "It is, and God did it."

In the days, months, and years that followed, the Lord taught Lori and me how to love each other and launched us into marriage ministry to help other couples. In addition, He saved all three of our precious girls. We've been *re*-married now for twenty-two years, and it just keeps getting better and better! The Bible says in Luke 1:37, "For with God, nothing will be impossible." My family and I are living proof of that truth.

"Daddy, it's a miracle," and I agreed!

We will never be able to fix whatever the "it" is in our lives that needs repair. I encourage you to call on the One who told me, "I fixed what you broke!"

—SCOTT & LORI DIX

Food for Thought

What seems impossible in your life right now? Maybe it's a struggling marriage where you no longer feel love towards your spouse. Perhaps you are addicted to alcohol, drugs, or pornography, which are destroying your life. Ponder these questions to determine if there is an area in your marriage that needs the loving repair of our heavenly Father.

- Do you understand that you are sinful and broken and need "fixing?" Reference Exodus 20:1-17, 1 John 3:4, Romans 3:23 and 6:23.
- What have you tried to fix in your life but can't? Is it a relationship, an addiction, anger, bitterness, financial trouble, something you feel you can't forgive?
- Have you ever cried out to God and asked him to fix you and the other broken things in your life? He loves you and is waiting for you to do just that! Reference Romans 5:8, 10:9-10, 13, 1 Timothy 2:4 and Matthew 7:7-8, 1 Peter 5:7.

Father, I thank you that you love me and that you can do the impossible. I come to you and ask you to reveal to me what is broken and in need of fixing in my life. Help me trust you and allow you to do the work you want to do in me and my life. In Jesus' name. Amen.

JUST WHO IS RESPONSIBLE HERE?

RECENTLY, it occurred to me that I have always felt responsible for the whole world. And I do mean RESPONSIBLE!

It started in high school after I became a Christian. No one ever held an election about being the "responsible" one. And no one else seemed to want the job to be the responsible one. So it fell to me. How could I turn down a job that no one else wanted?

I have always been responsible for hanging around anyone remotely scampering toward trouble. And suppose that someone finds trouble behind my back despite my warnings. In those instances, it has been my responsibility to provide either encouragement or punishment to initiate their total and faithful repentance. In other words, I have understood that I'm not God the Father or Jesus, God the Son and Savior. But at times, I've been glad to mimic, and indeed usurp, the duties of the Holy Spirit!

At times, if I thought my husband was getting out of line, then BAM! I could pull out my Bible quicker than any gunslinger could a pistol! And since it was all based on my responsibility to bring judgment, if I had to prooftext to make my point, that would surely be overlooked as a cost of the job.

If my kids pushed the boundaries of my beliefs and I needed to feel in control, once again, BLAMMO! But look at all the confession and forgiveness I kept them from going through!

But now I see it clearly. Satan the Accuser, once again and always, is telling me as he did with Adam and Eve that I can be as God—God the Holy Spirit.

I admit that I am not God the Father, Son, or Holy Spirit. Believing so is a lie from the pits of hell. And I'm not responsible for the actions (or sins) of the world—just those between me and my Heavenly Father.

Today, when I'm even tempted to carry the responsibility of others, I remind myself that this can be to my detriment. God gave us free will to choose. But God will not force himself on anyone. And as an overly responsible person, I am violating this principle and getting in God's way.

I am interfering in God's plan when I take on the responsibility of others.

We are responsible *to* people, but not *for* them. True maturity as a Christian helps us understand that part of God's design is to help people make good choices through success and failure. I am interfering in God's plan when I take on the responsibility of others.

—KELLY RANDLES LANIER

Food for Thought

Biblical accountability is essential for Christian growth. When we take on the sins of others or attempt to correct them through our judgment and preaching, we remove the opportunity for that person to answer for their own actions. That is the work of the Holy Spirit, who searches all things and knows all things.

Read Romans 14:12. What does it say about individual accountability?

Review 2 Corinthians 5:10. Who will appear before the judgment seat of Christ?

In the future, when you feel the weight of someone else's responsibility, consider the three "C's:"

- Did I "**cause**" this? *If not, then I'm not responsible.*
- Can I "**control**" this? *If not, it's not my responsibility.*
- Can I "**cure**" it? *If not, then it's not my responsibility.*

Release them to God and allow Him to restore them.

Lord, I humble myself before You. Holy Spirit, I am sorry for the sin of mocking Your Godhood with my silly, feeble attempts to replace You! Amen.

LET IT GO

> *Do not let the sun go down while you are still angry.*
> Ephesians 4:26 NLT

DO YOU EVER feel like something is just "off" as a couple? Something is brewing or festering, and you can't quite figure it out? Or maybe you know EXACTLY what the conflict is . . .

MAKE THE TIME

What happens to all of us as couples at one time or another is we get busy, and we just sweep it under the rug.
Then things begin to fester and grow because we didn't deal with it at the time.

MAKE THE TIME

As couples, we need to make regular time to have an open conversation to discuss:
- ✓ Is everything OK?
- ✓ Can we do better in a certain area?
- ✓ Have I hurt you in any way?
- ✓ Is there a problem?

Discuss it.

Resolve it or try to come to a solution or a decision.

Ask forgiveness.

Give forgiveness.

Move forward.

And then . . . LET IT GO! (*Truly, just like the song!*)

LET IT GO. LET IT GO.

Or if you prefer Taylor, then . . .

SHAKE IT OFF. SHAKE IT OFF.

LET IT GO

(*Can you tell I am a musician? LOL!*)

If it is possible, as far as it depends on you,
live at peace with everyone.
Romans 12:18 NIV

We don't want to lose or waste a day.

'Cuz we don't get it back.

LET IT GO

—TAMMY ATEN

Food for Thought

One of the most challenging things to do from a mental perspective is letting go. Sometimes, it's just plain hard! Letting go involves releasing emotional attachments, unmet expectations, or feeling interconnected to something. Spiritually, God cannot put something in our hand (or heart) if we hold onto something else.

Letting go can be a very freeing experience if we will trust the Lord. Review the key points below, which are launch points for letting go. Trust the Lord to enlighten you, particularly if you like to hold on to things that aren't right for you or may not be suitable for you.

- ✓ Forgive them, even if they haven't yet apologized.
- ✓ Put the care of yourself as a priority. Sometimes, you must move away from the situation to remain healthy.
- ✓ Practice acceptance. It may be time for a reset if the item can't be fixed or the circumstance can't be changed.
- ✓ Remain optimistic.
- ✓ Open your hands and allow God to replace what you have released.

LOSS OF A DREAM

I WAS HIDING out in the ladies' choir room, tears streaming down my face. My thoughts cried out, God, why not us? We have teenagers in our youth group getting pregnant and a woman in our church who calls her children 'rugrats' and doesn't even want them. We love you and are serving you. Why can't we get pregnant?

But as the choir sang Trust and Obey behind me and I listened to the words of that hymn, I was reminded of a Bible verse I'd recently been prompted to memorize:

> *Though the fig tree does not bud and there are no grapes on the vines, though the olive crop fails and the fields produce no food, though there are no sheep in the pen and no cattle in the stalls, yet I will rejoice in the LORD, I will be joyful in God my Savior. The Sovereign LORD is my strength; he makes my feet like the feet of a deer, he enables me to tread on the heights.*
> Habakkuk 3:17-19 NIV

The prophet was speaking of a time when the people were surely distraught. There was no food and no prospect of income-producing crops or livestock. The passage doesn't tell us what

God did for these people in response to their bleak situation. But it does tell us what we need to do.

The situation looked hopeless...yet the people rejoiced in the Lord. And that's what we must do, as well. We must rejoice in the Lord, remembering He is our Sovereign Lord. He is sovereign over our situation!

So that's what I did. I reminded myself that God is good, He loves me, and He is sovereign. He will decide where our babies will come from—either from our own bodies or how God expands His family through adoption. And we would trust Him in it.

Maybe you haven't faced infertility. But I bet somewhere or somehow, life hasn't turned out like you thought it would. Perhaps you faced a divorce. Maybe a loved one died prematurely. Maybe you had a financial loss or a career loss. Perhaps you or someone you love lost their health. Maybe you had a prodigal child, or they may still be a prodigal.

God is good, He loves me, and He is sovereign.

All of these situations involve the loss of a dream. You had a dream or a fantasy about everything turning out one way. And now it's turned out another way.

Whatever dreams have been lost or wherever the life you planned took a detour, it all boils down to our choices: how we choose to relate to God and how we choose to relate to each other. In our situation, we decided early on (when we weren't getting pregnant and started the crazy journey of inviting a team of doctors into our bedroom!) to draw even closer to God. We deliberately chose to praise Him, trust Him, and be joyful amidst pain and confusion.

We also decided not to blame. From the start, we decided it wouldn't be "my fault" or "your fault." We were in this together, and our situation wouldn't pull us apart. And since then, we've continued to strive to choose and think of "we" over "me" in our marriage.

—DWAINA (AND PATRICK) SIX

Food for Thought

Loss comes in many forms. But the loss of a dream has as much impact as a physical death. It involves the end of something that you hoped or planned for. But perhaps, as Christians, we should view a broken dream as a brand-new beginning.

God's plan may involve something even better for you. Allow your hope to be resurrected into a new plan or purpose with the Lord's leading. Consider the following thoughts as you take on a new outlook in response to the loss of a dream.

- The loss of a plan or goal doesn't change who you are. It may have changed your work status or position in life, but at the core, you are still a child of the most High God. Be proud of that, knowing that you are a person of great worth to God.

- The Bible assures us that *all things* work for good, not just the good things themselves. Understand that God gathers the fragments during lost desires and unrealized ambitions so that nothing may be lost. Be excited about what He will do with the remnants of a lost dream as He works it for good in your life.

- God loves to give good gifts to His children. Just because one dream didn't work out doesn't mean that God doesn't have other gifts for you. Keep trusting Him to work out His way, His will, in His time.

LOVE AND RESPECT—A MATTER OF LIFE AND DEATH

I LOVE MY three precious grandchildren, Hunter, Cooper, and Aubrey. I love to play with them in their playhouse, sit and watch a movie together, eat ice cream, or just let them beat me up as we wrestle on the bed. Looking into their eyes, watching them smile, and hearing their laugh brings joy beyond words to me. I often think back and consider that things could have been drastically different.

Their amazing mom, Jennifer, is our oldest daughter, and their wonderful dad, Tyler, is our son-in-law. Back when they were dating, they were going through a rough period. During that time, I noticed that Jen began talking disrespectfully to Tyler; my wife, Lori, also saw it. We were concerned as it wasn't a one-time occurrence; it was repetitive.

So, I sat down with Jen, shared our concerns with her, and then shared some verses from God's word about how we are to speak and treat each other. Proverbs 18:21 says, "Life and death are in the power of the tongue." Ephesians 5:33 says, "The husband must love his wife as he loves himself, and the wife must respect her husband."

Although they were not married yet, we knew their relationship was heading in that direction. So, I shared with Jen that if she wanted to marry him, she must respectfully speak to him. Otherwise, he would have enough at some point, and there would be no marriage. She admitted that she had been frustrated about some things but didn't realize she had been doing that so much. She thanked me for bringing it to her attention; we prayed together, and I never saw the behavior again.

Fast forward a couple of years, Tyler calls me and asks me to go to lunch at Saltgrass Steakhouse, and he's paying, so of course, I went—and ate a lot! During this unforgettable lunch, Tyler asked my permission for Jennifer's hand in marriage. I gave him our full blessing and told him that Lori and I knew he was "the one" the first time we met him. We had a beautiful time together, and then he said, "Can I ask you a question."

I said, "Ask me anything."

Then he said, "What did you say to her?"

I immediately knew what he was referring to, so I shared the conversation Jen and I had a couple of years earlier.

Tyler told me that he and Jen were struggling during that time and didn't know if they would make it. Then he said, "You had a conversation with her, and everything changed."

I then teared up and told him about the kind of woman he was marrying. Jen is a woman who is serious about following Jesus Christ. We brought something to her attention, and she repented, and we have never seen the behavior again. Jennifer told me later that after our conversation, she wrote Tyler a letter telling him 100 things she admired and respected about him as a man.

Jennifer and Tyler were united in marriage on July 20, 2013. I will never forget the divine glow as I walked my beautiful daughter down the aisle to Tyler. Since then, the Lord has blessed us and Tyler's family with Hunter, Cooper, and Aubrey.

Often, the Lord shows you things you never could see with your eyes, changing you forever. He did that to me when I recently read a passage in Genesis, chapter 20.

In this chapter, Abimelech, King of Gerar, intends to take and sleep with Sarah, Abraham's wife, whom Abraham tried to pass off as his sister. The Lord prevented him from doing so, coming to him in a dream and telling him to give her back. Abimelech repented and did as the Lord said, giving Abraham money, cattle, and servants.

> *Often, the Lord shows you things you never could see with your eyes.*

Then, it states a very interesting thing in verses 17-18. "So Abraham prayed to God, and God healed Abimelech, his wife, and his female servants. Then they bore children, for the Lord had closed up all the wombs of the house of Abimelech because of Sarah, Abraham's wife."

Here's what the Lord revealed to me when reading this. Repentance will always bring life in various forms; refusal to repent will always bring death in various forms. God showed me that if my daughter Jennifer had not repented for the way she was speaking to Tyler, it would have been the death of their relationship.

But she did repent, bringing life in Hunter, Cooper, and Aubrey—my grandchildren! So when I look into the wondrous eyes of my grandchildren and hear them say, "Papa, I luz you," I reflect back and thank God that I have an amazing daughter who chose to repent. And God blessed that decision with the gift of life. Oh, the goodness of God!

— SCOTT DIX

Food for Thought

What is the environment of your marriage? Husbands, do you love your wife through words and actions? Wives, are you respecting your husband in both words and actions? As a couple, share a time when your spouse did or said something that made you feel truly loved. Then, share a time when they said or did something where you didn't feel loved; express how that impacted you. Receive the comments with appreciation and understanding, not with negativity or in a defensive posture.

Are you "breathing life" (loving words that build up, edify, encourage) or "breathing death" (words that tear down or are negative, critical) on each other? Practice creative ways to breathe life into each other and watch how it affects your spouse and the environment of your marriage. Read and memorize key verses such as Proverbs 18:21 or Ephesians 5:33.

What areas in your marriage need repentance? Remember, it's a matter of life and death!

Father, please help the environment of our marriage to be warm, loving, and respectful. Please reveal any areas that are not pleasing to you in thought, word, or action and help us correct them. May we walk in the Spirit, breathing life into each other. In Jesus' name. Amen.

MARRIAGE IN THE DICTIONARY

I LOOKED UP the word "marriage" in the dictionary. The Google Docs and Britannica versions say that marriage is a noun. I would not fare too well getting into a war of words with the people smart enough to write the dictionary. And, here it comes . . . but . . . I'm not sure they got that one right.

You see, I have been married, I am married now, and most of the people I know are married. None of us are living a noun. In my experience, marriage is much more a verb than a noun.

Consider this point for my case: Get married, do absolutely nothing, and then count the times you can continue to tell people you are still married.

> **Marriage is an action verb;**
> **perhaps *the* action verb.**

And because marriage is a verb, the acts do not always go well. Have you ever watched movies or documentaries about the Apollo space program? Everyone remembers the line from those movies: "Houston, we have a problem." The scramble is on. When hearing this famous line, I always think that it would have been fun to hear one astronaut say to the other, "Wow, I wish I hadn't left the duct tape on the launching pad."

Is marriage so different? How often in our marriages do we internally think, *Houston, we have a problem.* But this can be helpful. For example, marriage can teach us how to define a crisis. That's another devotion for another day.

Because marriage is a verb, the acts sometimes go better than we could imagine. When you are given a second chance at love at a time in life when you doubted if that would happen, everything can seem better than imagined. Here's a life lesson: God is bigger than our imagination. And with Him present in our marriage, the chance for blessings increases God fold because He is not limited to what we can comprehend.

With marriage being a verb, there is action in our relationship. And action causes friction. This is where I could take this analogy too far and get in trouble, but I won't. The truth is, it is better with God in control instead of between the sources of friction. The amount of friction, the heat produced by the friction, and the wear and tear over time that friction causes have to be handled with a better perspective, better eyes, and better hands than the sources.

Laughingly, I have not received a call from Wikipedia to correct the grammatical placement mistake concerning marriage. It's almost like no one cares what I know. *Imagine that?*

But I can say this for certain: One day, Christ is going to come for His bride. And when He does, in that marriage, we are going to be held accountable for what we have done (as in the *verb*), not for what they call us (as in the *noun*).

—KIM LANIER

Food for Thought

Often, couples exclaim with excitement, "We're getting married!" But marriage isn't something you *get*. It is something you *do*.

Over time, a marriage relationship can become mundane or lack excitement. This typically occurs when your marriage becomes something you *have* rather than something you *do*.

Be intentional about your daily interactions as a couple to keep the intrigue alive. Keep doing the things you did together when you first married.

Revelation 2:4 teaches, "But I have this against you: You have abandoned your first love." This scripture means, "You stopped doing the things you did when we first fell in love."

List the exciting things you and your spouse did together early in your marriage. Then check the ones that are still part of your routine today. Is it time to incorporate some of your former customs back into your relationship?

e.g., *Took long walks together 2-3x a week*

[ ] _____

[ ] _____

[ ] _____

[ ] _____

[ ] _____

MARRIAGE MATTERS

YOUR MARRIAGE MATTERS is what I mean to say. Especially in today's culture, your traditional, God-created relationship as man and wife matters. More today than ever. Allow me to give you just two reasons why:

Until the day we die, Tammy and I will quote words from a man we knew as a modern-day John the Baptist—the late and greatly missed Jon Randles. As keynotes for most of our Three2One Marriage events, Jon & his wife, Kelly, taught this first truth as key, "Your marriage is your second greatest testimony."

After your personal relationship with Jesus Christ, your marriage testimony becomes your second most important story. Yes, people still notice you as an individual. But there's always the knowledge that you are now married and united as one with your spouse. You have a ring on your finger. People start to listen & look at you differently. They watch how you treat your husband or wife in public. Your friends watch, your coworkers watch, your church watches, your family watches & especially your kids watch (and we know they see the real deal at home)!

In Ephesians 5 (Vs. 22-33), Paul states that Christian marriage is a *mystery*. But one thing he knows for sure is that the union between a husband & wife *represents* Christ & the Church. Whoa! That's a sobering reality. *Your marriage is what the world around you sees as a picture of Jesus & His Bride.* So, no pressure. Just know that your marriage is testifying to something, 24/7. It is loudly speaking to your world, and it doesn't matter if you are in your first or fifth marriage. What matters to God and others is where you are at this moment.

The second reason your marriage matters is that it is your LEGACY. You are already someone's ancestor! *Hmmm...that sounds old.* Is anyone here interested in family trees or ancestry? Even if you're not into that, you are *on* and *in* a family tree—several trees. And those we leave behind will carry on the ways we lived, mainly by observation. But also by having our genes. That can also be a sobering & even scary reality.

> *You are on and in a family tree—several trees.*

Not only your children but all those you have ever influenced will tend to do things the way you did. The Old Testament speaks of the sins of the father visiting the third and even fourth generations *of those who hate Me.* Just look at those who came before you. And without Jesus, what do you sometimes see? That's why your children and their children need to love Jesus; that's the legacy we want to leave.

My Dad, whom I respected for how he provided for and parented us, sometimes told me (his firstborn), "Sherman, do what I say, not what I do." I didn't really know what that meant at the time. But my father knew I was watching him and learning things he hoped I wouldn't.

Hopefully, you know that doesn't work. Our kids hear what we say and may not be listening, but they will definitely *do* what we do. So, the older I got, the more I realized there were some things I didn't want to follow me into my own marriage and parenting journey.

We've all at least thought this at one time or another: *Oh, I will never be like that!* Or we've thought, *I will never be—, say—, or do—that!* Well, good luck!

To this day, when I do or say something that would have sounded or looked like my raising, before I can even condemn myself, my sweet wife says, "Well, that was Hobbs!" Ugh. No matter how much I don't want to repeat my ancestral ways, I forget that I have their genes.

But thankfully, I also have the Holy Spirit. And the Holy Spirit trumps those ancestral genes when I allow Him.

So, I remind myself that *it matters* while living everyday life in front of whoever's watching. What they observe will surface at some point in their lives. And prayerfully, we will see the fruit of our actions in them.

"Lord, God, I pray. Let it be only the good fruit they take from me. Amen."

Likewise, urge the younger men to be self-controlled. Show yourself in all respects to be a model of good works, and in your teaching, show integrity, dignity, and sound speech that cannot be condemned so that an opponent may be put to shame, having nothing evil to say about us.

Titus 2:6-8 ESV

—SHERMAN ATEN

Food for Thought

Observational learning is a phenomenon that helps us interact with others. Teachers, parents, coworkers, peers, and siblings influence through modeled and repetitive behaviors. In the Christian faith, we call this "discipleship." We have the responsibility to guard our walk and talk. 1 Timothy 4:16 says, "Keep a close watch on yourself and on your teaching. Stay true to what is right, and God will save you and those who hear you." What we do and how we relate to others demonstrates the love and Godly example of Jesus.

Who has been placed in your path that closely observes your behavior? Name people below, including your spouse, children, fellow church members, or others in your sphere of influence. Commit to praying for each name over the next ten days.

Ask the Lord to show you areas of weakness where you aren't modeling behaviors that demonstrate the love of God. Allow Him, through the assistance of the Holy Spirit, to help you be more mindful of your actions and teachings.

_____

_____

_____

_____

_____

_____

MASCULINITY, NOT PASSIVITY

MEN WHO DON'T struggle with tyranny often swing over to the other side—passivity. It is a subtle and sneaky tune that leads to corrupt masculinity. The book of Genesis demonstrates the first sin in the Bible isn't partaking of the forbidden fruit. It's Adam's passivity.

> *When the woman saw that the fruit of the tree was good for food and pleasing to the eye, and also desirable for gaining wisdom, she took some and ate it. She also gave some to her husband, who was with her, and he ate it.*
>
> Genesis 3:6 NIV

As you read, Adam is silent when Eve listens to the Serpent. He's passive as he listens to Eve. He is complicit when he takes and eats the fruit while in physical proximity. Adam is right there with her, standing on the sidelines, sitting on his hands, while things go south.

We dance to this same tune when our employees, best friends, girlfriends, wives, and children go south. We throw up our hands and say, "**Not my problem!**" or one of these common phrases: "I'm too tired. Not today. I'm tapped out. My job is stressful. I solve problems all week at work. I'm depressed. I deserve to sit

SHERMAN & TAMMY ATEN

on the couch, veg, and disengage. When I refuse to join the dance, I leave my people to fend for themselves and on their own."

Eventually, after saying "not my problem" long enough, the things entrusted to me begin falling apart. So, I sling another passive phrase, "**Not my fault!**" This is Adam's first reaction to His passivity.

Adam feels guilty and ashamed, so he designs clothing for himself and Eve, and then they hide (Genesis 3:9-12). He then blames it on Eve. Not surprisingly, the word blame is spelled "B. Lame." Instead of man-ing up, Adam says, "This woman you gave me . . .." Not only is He blaming Eve, but he's blaming God. He's saying, "It's *your* fault, and it's *her* fault."

The essence of this passivity lands on the final phrase, "**Not my responsibility!**" I'm busy. I'm killing it at work. I'm a scratch golfer . . . you get the drift.

> *Masculinity is when we dance to God's music.*

These three phrases are the holy trinity of passive masculinity. Passivity can strike in financial, marital, emotional, vocational, parental, or spiritual arenas.

Men, where did we go wrong? We don't know what healthy masculinity looks like! Until the right song is downloaded into our playlist, we will keep switching musical tracks between tyranny and passivity. The people that will pay the most are the people we care about the most. And sadly, we don't even know what's up.

What will restore our manhood? Masculinity is when we dance to God's music. The way to regain masculinity (what we've lost in Adam) is to discover a vibrant beat we can follow. The score behind the composition is healthy masculinity and is God-designed masculinity. Find a mentor. Find a church. Listen hard.

Wives play a big role here, as well. Encourage him when he steps up and gives it a shot, no matter how small the effort. Tell him how you admire and respect his attempt. Remind him you are in his corner. There is a strong possibility he'll do it again.

—DR. JOE STEWART

Food for Thought

Noted author and theologian Joe Rigney once said, *"Masculinity is about taking responsibility for the physical, emotional, and spiritual safety of those in our care."* Masculinity ties directly to God's calling.

It comes naturally when men sacrificially follow after Christ, who is the ground for masculinity.

Christ took Adam's insufficiency and sin to the cross and arose with a new plan for man. Whereas Adam was passive and irresponsible, Christ became the example who protects, defends, and provides for those in His care.

Of the three attributes of Adam, which one do you struggle with the most?

Which of the three attributes of the new Adam do you need to work on the most?

OLD ADAM:
- Not my problem.
- Not my fault.
- Not my responsibility.

NEW ADAM (IN CHRIST):
- I will protect.
- I will defend.
- I will provide.

MASCULINITY, NOT TYRANNY

TWO-STEPPING leads men to twirl with a twisted enemy in one of two ways: 1) Tyranny or 2) Passivity. We discussed Adam and his passivity in the previous devotional, so let's address tyranny now.

Tyranny occurs when a man abuses his command to co-rule with God like a king. It's unplugging the headphones to go rogue with unchecked and unbridled power and authority.

> *To the woman he said, "I will make your pains in childbearing very severe; with painful labor you will give birth to children. Your desire will be for your husband, and he will rule over you."*
>
> Genesis 3:16 NIV

The verse above is hard to define, but it's a definite transition in tempo because of the fall of humanity. Man becomes a domineering tyrant instead of a loving servant. It's a tune playing on repeat as virility proves masculinity.

This theory is ingrained in some cultures as a strength (along with the mantra, "I don't need anyone's help"). But really, it's not a strength but a casualty. Satan uses the liner notes in Genesis to produce chaos, unravel relationships, cause violence, and bring death. Alienation ensues from one another, from our creator, and from nature itself, and what men were called to "cultivate" becomes cursed.

It's all too common. A large minority of women live in a home where there's abuse. Tyranny is controlling, selfish, aggressive, and abusive. It tries to remake those around you into a manufactured image rather than into the image of God.

With tyranny, Dads dictate the dance to the 'nth degree and exasperate their children by coming down hard on them. Husbands threatened by the strength or competence of their wives beat them down with words and wounds.

And sadly, every man is capable of dancing to the tune of tyranny. This includes pastors with power, coaches with a whistle, entrepreneurs with a checkbook, and husbands with a tongue! We probably operate out of tyranny more often than we think. It unravels fast and dark, and we go to war against those around us rather than join the battle for them.

Early on, I oppressed my wife. I wanted to control her instead of captivate her. I hoped to remake her into my image instead of allowing her to beautifully reflect God's image.

I'm thankful that I accepted God's call against tyranny and chose intentionality and vulnerability. That involves being a "man's man." Perfect masculinity is on display through Jesus. He's the most masculine man who ever lived. To avoid the cruel ways of tyranny, men must walk and talk and live like Jesus.

—DR. JOE STEWART

Food for Thought

There are several root causes for tyranny in a marriage:

- Insecurity
- Loss of control
- Jealousy
- Incompatible beliefs
- Lack of respect or value towards the other

And it is cloaked in many forms, such as overprotectiveness, gaslighting, bullying, or downright dominance and control. But this behavior cannot (and should not) be tolerated in a Christian home. Our example should be Jesus Christ, who gave himself up for His bride (check out Ephesians 5:25).

If you observe any of the behaviors below in your relationship, it's time to ask the Lord for His help in releasing them.

- Justification of your inappropriate actions
- Rationalization when you know you've done wrong
- Assuming a victim mentality for every disagreement
- Ignoring your spouse altogether
- Feeling that you are better than your spouse or others.

Lord, I humbly ask you to create a clean heart and a right spirit toward you and my marriage. Cleanse my prideful heart and help me be attuned to the leading of your Holy Spirit. In Jesus' name. Amen.

MAY I HAVE YOUR AUTOGRAPH?

I LOVED THAT SCENE in the Cowboys locker room when Jimmy Johnson shouted, "How 'Bout Them Cowboys!" after beating the San Francisco 49ers in the 1992 NFC Championship Game. They clobbered the Buffalo Bills in Super Bowl XXVII in Pasadena two weeks later.

We love the Dallas Cowboys; our kids grew up watching games every Sunday. We would even go out in the yard and run plays together. Our youngest daughter, Brianna, often wears a tee shirt that says, "My Dad taught me about Jesus and pass interference."

Little did I know that those Sundays were developing a passion in Brianna. She loved the game and wanted to cover it as a Sports Reporter. Brianna has a Sanguine personality; she is very outgoing, always uplifting, and just fun to be around. At Dallas Baptist University, she pursued a major in Broadcast Communications and discovered her talent for being in front of the camera and sharing people's stories.

Lori and I have always wanted our children to have a close relationship with God. Not just know *about* Him but have that vital, flourishing relationship where they encounter Him every day. I love Henry Blackaby's study, *Experiencing God*, as God changed my life through that study.

In it, Henry pulls truths or "realities" from scripture that show how God is always at work around us; He pursues a relationship with us and invites us to become involved with Him in his work. It teaches you how God speaks and how to recognize His voice as He reveals Himself, His purposes, and His ways.

According to Henry, when God communicates with us, it involves a "crisis of belief" where we must have faith, take action, and make necessary adjustments to participate in God's work. But as we do so and follow in obedience, we will experience God accomplishing His work through us.

We have always prayed that God would use us individually and as a family for his glory. I must admit that I was nervous when my baby girl wanted to get involved in the Sports/Entertainment industry, where there is so much ungodliness. However, that is precisely why God has placed her in it; she is to be salt and light in that industry. During college, we saw God reveal himself and his plan for her. For example, she applied for an internship with the Dallas Cowboys. She had been praying very generally for the Lord to put her where He wanted her, as she would do whatever He wanted her to do.

Then, one night at a DBU prayer meeting, a total stranger came up to Brianna and said, "I don't know if this means anything to you or not, but the Lord impressed upon me to tell you that if you want something you need to ask for it."

Brianna responded, "I know exactly what that means, and thank you for sharing that with me!" She went home and poured out her heart to the Lord, praying specifically for the internship. The next morning, she had a text for an interview, and ultimately, she got the position.

God worked through Brianna in amazing ways with that internship, and she experienced Him as He accomplished His work through her. I will let her describe in her own words one such memorable moment:

> *As a Game Day Event Presentation Intern in 2016 and for some of the game days, my job was to escort the trumpet player for the National Anthem, Freddie Jones. During one of the first games that season, I was his escort and got to be on the sideline for kickoff. The music began, and I started crying. The crowd was singing the Anthem in unison, and I got chills. I looked up and felt the presence of God, and He spoke to me. He said as clear as day, "Brianna, look where you are. Look where I have placed you. I am faithful; will you trust me?" I will never be able to forget that moment; I knew I was where he wanted me. Never doubt God or what He is capable of; there is a reason He puts desires in your heart.*

Psalm 37:4 says, "Delight yourself in the Lord and he will give you the desires of your heart." The internship then opened the door for her to work as a reporter and writer for D210 Sports, covering, you guessed it—The Dallas Cowboys! She attends team practices, press conferences, and locker rooms. And on game days, she sits in the press box analyzing/reporting on the game.

I have witnessed her bring comfort to those facing challenges in life, whether it be the loss of a sibling or a child or just needing encouragement. She has talked about her faith with Hall of Fame Legends, the security guards, fellow reporters, and media personnel.

The most gratifying moment for me was when she spoke at a mother/daughter banquet in the Metroplex. Brianna spoke to a packed room that included everyone from young girls, ladies in high school and college, and their moms. I watched with stunning admiration at how she laid out her life with total transparency in front of these ladies. Brianna spoke about her thoughts, plans, and dreams and how those changed with the loss of her sister. She talked about experiencing God during that time and how it changed her outlook from then on.

Brianna told them, "Since then, I have vowed to live each day with a smile on my face and pursue my passions. I know how brief life is, and so I dreamed big. God has a way of moving mountains and makes what seems impossible possible." She challenged these ladies to embrace God's plan for their lives and live it out with passion, to experience God every step of the way. As I scanned the room, I knew God fully captured these ladies' hearts while speaking through Brianna.

After her talk, a beautiful nine-year-old girl came up to Brianna and spoke to her for a minute. The little girl said, "May I have your autograph?" Brianna hugged her and wrote her a loving, encouraging note. At that moment, it tied everything together for me: the passion, the purpose, the path. God gave Brianna the passion to go down that path to use her to reach people for his glory.

—SCOTT DIX

Food for Thought

Throughout the scriptures, we are encouraged to ask God for what we want. God hears our requests and delights in answering them. But it requires a personal, in-depth relationship with Him.

1. Do you trust God to speak to your children and direct their path, or do you try to determine their path? Read Proverbs 3:5-6.

2. Have you discussed with your children what they are passionate about? Consider a date night with your child as a wonderful time to discuss their passions, hopes, and dreams.

3. Have you "experienced" God? Or do you only know about him? Consider picking up Henry Blackaby's study titled *Experiencing God—Knowing and Doing the Will of God*. Go through it together as husband and wife.

Father, thank you for loving and pursuing us! Please help us experience you individually, in our marriages, and in our families. In Jesus' name. Amen.

MY MAN

> *When I found him whom my soul loves*
> *I held him, and would not let him go.*
> Song of Solomon 3:4 ESV

I MARRIED my very best friend—the love of my life.
I'm still very much "in love."

We met as university students. We always wanted to be together.
And we still do after 38 years!
That has never changed.
When you've found your forever person, you've found them.

I love his strength.
I love his fearlessness.
I love that he steps one foot in front of the other, even when he's hurting.
I love his bold leadership, although he also asks my thoughts.
I love his constants!
- ✓ Quiet time in his chair with his coffee
- ✓ A bike ride after that
- ✓ His nightly rituals

I love that he loves God more than me.
I love that he's conscious about his health and mine, too.

I love that he's still the closest thing to Jesus I'll ever see in this world.

I love seeing his eyes light up and his face change at the sight of any of his g-babies (melts my heart).

I. Love. Him.

—TAMMY ATEN

Food for Thought

Have you told your spouse "your things?" You know—the little things that we sincerely love about them?

Compose a list of the ordinary and the *extra*ordinary things you adore in your spouse. Then, carve out time to share your list with them.

A MYSTERY AND A MIRACLE

MARRIAGE—Paul said it was a mystery! But for sure, it's a miracle. Jesus said:

> *As You sent Me into the world,*
> *I have sent them into the world.*
> John 17:18 NIV

Biblical marriage is a remarkable union of two individuals. There is guidance in the scripture concerning how this bond of two bodies, minds, hearts, and souls is supposed to be. Marriage is sacred enough to God that He instructs husbands to love their wives with the same love God has for His church. And yet, there seems to be a severe lack of biblical examples to show us exactly what He means.

Adam and Eve started things rolling by loving each other enough to introduce all humanity to death from sin. Abraham and Sarah are considered a great example of marriage, and all they did was bring a third partner to the party, with Sarah turning the kids against their dad. Or take King David. He loved Abigail—at least more than all his other wives.

The list of challenging and mysterious relationships in the Bible is relatively long. Oh, sure, a couple or two seem to get it right. For example, in Joseph and Mary, where he faithfully stands by his wife, even after discovering she was pregnant through an immaculate conception. But why are there so few others?

Just so you know, I would rather go into battle with 10,000 men than 300. I would not send a baby to do a King's job, and I would not pick twelve mismatched misfits to carry on my plans. Just sayin'.

Therefore, it has occurred to me that maybe marriage fits into the same category as miracles and other actions that can only be explained as divine interventions. Perhaps marriage is a consecrated lifestyle, but we just don't do it well.

I think the first time I ever heard the phrase "You may be the only Christ that someone ever sees" was from the pulpit of a Southern Baptist home missionary. As a kid, I would rather they see me play baseball because I really wanted to be a major leaguer.

But as I have grown in life and marriage, I have come to understand the significance of Christian marriage in the eyes of the world. My spouse is no less than a miraculous gift. Our marriage is no less than our representation of our Savior. Our love for each other is an example of His love for us. I do not know why He would, and I am not sure marriage is the way I would show my love to the world.

Then again, isn't that just like something God would do?

—KIM LANIER

Food for Thought

In the Bible, there are no "perfect" couples. And yet, God has given us marriage as part of His divine plan to help us become more like Christ. Someone once said, "A perfect marriage is just two imperfect people who won't give up on each other."

The most perfect of unions is that between Christ and His church. And we are to use the example of Christ to rid all selfishness, envy, insecurity, doubt, and the host of other sins we bring into our marriage.

Rather than comparing your marriage to another marriage here on earth, consider the mysterious union of Christ and His Bride. That is how we should behave toward one another. Husbands and wives should imitate God's intended relationship based on the model of Christ and the church.

Below are some attributes that Christ has toward His Bride. Which ones cause you to stumble within your relationship? Ask the Lord to help *perfect* that which concerns you (Psalm 138:8).

- Humility
- Yielding
- Attentiveness
- Overlooking Faults
- Responsibility for actions
- Provision
- Support – Emotionally, Physically and Spiritually
- Reverence

NEVER GONNA LET YOU GO

Have you seen the one my heart loves? Scarcely had
I passed them when I found the one my heart loves.
I held him and would not let him go till I had
brought him to my mother's house,
to the room of the one who conceived me.
Song of Solomon 3:3b-4 NIV

IT'S GOOD TO REMEMBER the various "whens" of life. Like the 80s, when music was, is, and always shall be the greatest of all times. *Why, even my millennial son & daughter agree.* You may not, but you have the right to be mistaken. Ha!

Take Sergio Mendez's *Never Gonna Let You Go.* That was the first duet Tammy & I ever sang. We weren't even dating then—at least, not yet.

Tammy & I met as music students at a West Texas private school, Wayland Baptist University. Neither of us had planned to go there. After high school, my plan was to "go west, young man," to California along with my buddy, Guy Penrod. We had both received vocal scholarships to Pacific Coast Baptist Bible College in high school and thought we were all set!

Guy and his family had moved to Hobbs, NM, in 1978, where his father pastored Temple Baptist Church. One day, I just happened to be in the music building and was asked to accompany a new student auditioning for the Acapella Choir. The choir was led by my spiritual & musical mentor, Ben Canfield, or "Mr. C," as we called him. (*I could make this devotional about Mr. C, but I won't.*) During the next three years, the choir student (Guy) and I became best friends, and I probably spent more time at his house than my own.

I wasn't from a Christian family, so the Penrods sort of took me in. And as it turned out, neither one of us went to California. God led Guy to Liberty University, and I was offered a better scholarship to Wayland. I'm glad Someone else was arranging my steps!

Tammy grew up as a P.K. (Pastor's Kid). Her mom & dad, Hollis & Jo Payne, were some of the most Godly and greatest generation teachers/pastors that West Texas has ever known. But like most preacher's kids, when it was time to leave for college, Tammy wanted to be farther than 45 minutes down the road. She had received a piano scholarship to North Texas State in Denton, and off she went—no more glass houses for her!

I'm glad Someone else was arranging my steps!

North Texas State was where musicians were made, and that was Tammy's dream. But again, someone else was in control. She became ill one semester and had to go home. She ended up where she said she wouldn't go, 45 minutes down the road to Wayland Baptist. Of course, she maintained that she was "just finishing up a semester," and this was *not* a permanent move.

But this school . . . hmmm . . . it was different! And, of course, God was changing my path simultaneously, and I arrived at Wayland the semester after Tammy did.

Fast forward to 1983 and the Spirit of America Singers & Band. That's where Tammy and I performed our first duet, *Never Gonna Let You Go*. At the time, I didn't realize I was singing this with (and *to*) my wife-to-be. God was giving us a little glimpse into His Word:

For I know the plans I have for you, plans to prosper
you and not to harm you.
Plans to give you a future and a hope.
Jeremiah 29:11 NIV

We sang this song most of the semester every time our group performed. The hormones raced every single time. To this day, we still sing it. Whenever it randomly comes up on the radio or a playlist, we have to stop whatever we're in the middle of doing. And by the time the chorus plays, we're trying to see through damp eyes.

You may not think you can sing, and you may not like the music of the 80s. But at some point, *Never Gonna Let You Go* has been *your* song, too. So, let's try a fun exercise.

Take a moment to clear your throat, review the words here, then look at each other. Maybe you feel a little slow dance sway while you sing this song to each other.

Ready? Get set. Go . . .

Never gonna let you go. I'm gonna hold you in my arms
forever. Gonna try and make up for the times I've hurt you
so. Gonna hold your body close to mine. From this day on,
we're gonna be together. I swear this time,
I'm never gonna let you go.

—SHERMAN ATEN

SHERMAN & TAMMY ATEN

Food for Thought

Have you ever stood on the side of a mountain or along a steep path and had the sensation that something was holding on to you? The Bible teaches that God will never leave us or forsake us (Deuteronomy 31:8). In other words, He's not going to let us go. When you put your hand in His, He's there forever—you can count on that.

What an example that provides for us as partners in marriage. Your spouse needs to feel you are holding on to them, no matter how bad life gets. You can sing the song to them consistently or express that you're holding on by repeating the phrases below.

- ✓ Thank you.
- ✓ You look beautiful/handsome.
- ✓ You are amazing.
- ✓ I am here if you need me.
- ✓ What can I do for you today?
- ✓ You make a difference in my life.
- ✓ Can I help you with that?
- ✓ I believe in you.
- ✓ My life is better with you in it.

134

A NEWLYWED... AGAIN!

AT SIXTY-FIVE years of age, I found myself as a newlywed again. I had been here before, but it was forty-six years earlier. My bride and I now had 83 years of cumulative marriage experience and knew more about losing spouses to pancreatic cancer than we wanted to recall!

We had both been praying about our futures and were both somehow surprised when God answered those prayers with each other. Now, we had to figure out marriage from a new perspective.

As I mentioned, I was 65 years *old,* and my bride was 62 years *young.* I had robbed the cradle and now had united this vibrant young woman with my arthritic joints. The physical aspects of this marriage would have to be dealt with. I had been a school administrator for many years, and my emotional tank was close to empty.

A prominent local church employed her as the leader of community benevolence. She brought emotions to everything. She was a writer, a speaker, and an intellectual. I made comments on social media. I took a break from teaching my church groups. She was a prayer warrior and worshipped on her knees. I had outkicked my coverage!

And we had our children, parents, and finances to deal with. There were decisions to make, like finding a place to live and deciding on furniture, dishes, and what looked good on the wall by the window. There were discussions about what's for dinner, the TV remote, and the thermostat. Of course, she looked good in everything; nothing made her look fat, and her hair was always perfect.

All the life changes that sixty-five years bring. Some blessings of sight, others of faith alone. Some beautiful memories and some things I wish I could forget.

We all change along life's way, but in marriage, God ordained a union that is as consistent as He is. So, in this blessed union, we must earn the faith of one another every day. And continually find hope in what you each will become. We must love each other with God's heart.

This. Is. Marriage.

But then again, so is learning to eat meatloaf that isn't cooked the way my mom made it!

—KIM LANIER

Food for Thought

Society often refers to the first year of marriage as a "honeymoon" or a period of harmony immediately following a marriage. It is typically a time when newlywed couples focus most, if not all, of their attention on each other. But once a career, kids, mortgages, and all the minutia of life come along, it's easy to redirect our focus from our spouse.

Does your marriage need a spark of "newly wed" again? Have you shifted your view from loving your spouse foremost to now attending to other priorities and needs? Is the harmony of your relationship fading?

If so, consider some ideas below to redirect your attention back to each other.

- Pull out your marriage license (if you can find it!) and recall the day you obtained it.
- Remember the events of your wedding day. What was your most memorable encounter?
- Try on your wedding dress/tux if they are still around. If not, pull out some old photos and reminisce.
- Recreate your very first date.
- Call someone who participated in your wedding and thank them for their support over the years.
- Each of you jot down the five most essential marriage tips you would give a couple today.
- Consider what you spent on your honeymoon. Is your budget farther along today? If so, give thanks to the Lord!

PERFECTION AND HOW TO ACHIEVE IT

> *For by one sacrifice He has made perfect forever*
> *those who are being made holy.*
> Hebrews 10:14 NIV

HAVE YOU EVER seen anything created by man that was perfect? If you put "perfect" on a plate and set it on the place settings at a large gathering, each person would find something they would change. We would never recognize perfection, even if it stared us in the face. We could kill it with criticism, cynicism, or even crucifixion.

So, let's begin by agreeing that perfection is in the beholder's eye. A beautiful mountain panorama may be the perfect setting for you, but another will long for the ocean. Or you believe the mountains are the ideal place for you until you live there for a while.

I can always recognize other people hopelessly searching for perfection or going from one thing to another to make themselves happy. Rolling my eyes, I silently think, *Tsk, Tsk,* because I'm not like that now. Being close to my family makes any place feel like home to me, and it takes a bulldozer to dig me out and put me somewhere else.

However, my pursuit of perfection was very destructive at one time in my life. It was a search for perfection within myself, leaving me full of anxiety, depression, and self-doubt.

Women, in general, are people pleasers and caregivers. To make everyone else happy, we strive toward giving perfection to everyone. Mothers are the worst at seeking perfection. It fills our waking thoughts and actions because we do it for our family.

We compare our efforts to other mothers who excel in homemade Halloween costumes, treats for school, and science projects. We strive to enroll our children in

Mothers are the worst at seeking perfection.

every activity within a 60-mile radius— musical lessons, karate, horseback riding, etc. Our goal is to provide everything they need so people will view us as excellent parents. Then comes the guilt when the inevitable happens because we can't do everything.

And striving for perfection doesn't stop at home. It is part of work outside the home. We can't escape!

I had to work outside the home for all kinds of reasons that aren't important to dwell on. So, I compared myself to every mother who got to spend more time with their children. Any night my son went to sleep without me tucking him in would rip my heart out, and guilt would take over.

It was a constant battle. I managed a family newspaper business while my husband served as a police officer—both demanding jobs with a lot of time commitment. Guilt consumed me when I was at work because I wasn't at home. At home, I worried about work and felt guilty about letting my co-workers down.

My guilt and striving for perfection were such a mess in my mind. Someone (*who prowls around like a roaring lion*) convinced me that Jesus would be disappointed in me. I wanted to do everything right to please Him.

Thankfully, I attended a spiritual retreat in a beautiful canyon outside Floydada, Texas. It took nothing short of a miracle to get me there away from my family. The first day, I worried about how the family and work were going to get along without me. But I didn't want to return home by the end of the four days! I wanted to stay in God's presence and bask longer in His love. And in all the time I spent with Jesus, not once did I hear, "I'm disappointed in you." All I heard was how much He loved me.

Jesus also revealed something I'll never forget, which is for everyone. He made it clear there was nothing I could *do* to make Him love me more. All He wanted from me was my love. And it didn't matter what I ended up *doing*. All that was important to Jesus was that I do it "FOR HIM."

Showing Jesus' love means laboring for Him in all that I do. It may sound difficult, but it will be the most liberating realization. Receiving Love from Jesus is just a matter of choosing to do so. Realizing you are forgiven for eternity after that decision removes the burden of trying to be perfect. Because you can't be, and best of all, you don't have to be.

Perfection will never come from me. It will always come from Him. I may never see how His perfection will manifest itself, but the person it is intended for will always see it if they choose.

—ALICE GILROY

Food for Thought

When we seek perfection in and of ourselves, we become human "doings" rather than human "beings" to find value. That is a vicious cycle that never ends. We can never do enough to find true worth. Consider these questions, and if the answer is "yes" to any, you may be caught in a perfection-trap.

Read Hebrews 10:14-18 and allow God to minister His release from perfection to your soul.

- Do you ever feel like you aren't good enough or that you are failing the people you care about? Where do you think those feelings are coming from? Do you find it hard to bring peace to your mind?
- Are you anxious and worried about everyone or everything around you? Do you feel like you have to fix it?
- Can you just relax each evening, although the "to-do" list may not have been completed?
- Are you too busy to spend daily time alone with Jesus?

Thank you, Jesus, for your life for us. Thank you for making the ultimate sacrifice so we could be made holy and blameless in our Father's eyes. Help me remember, Holy Spirit, that when I worry about not being good enough, I am forgetting the sacrifice already made for me. Help me find peace and rest in your arms. Help me remember there is nothing I can do that could make You love me more. Show me I have nothing to prove to you.

Remind me that it is not only impossible to work hard enough or long enough to "be better," but it is also totally unnecessary to try.

Your Word says the one sacrifice has made me perfect and that you will remember our sins no more. Thank you for your mercy and love. Amen.

PERMISSION TO LOVE (& HURT) ME

A PART OF marriage is giving someone else the power to hurt you and then trusting them for safety.

In school, we learned Maslow's hierarchy of needs. At the base of those needs are the things that literally keep us breathing, and then right on top of that base is the following need: the need for safety. The simplified explanation is that nothing else is possible; love, esteem, peace—without feeling safe. It is like discovering your lack of covering and trying to hide from God so He won't find out.

As it turns out, the person we should trust most with our safety is the same person we become the most vulnerable to. Giving someone permission to love us seems to require giving them the ability to hurt us as well. This thing is called "love."

> *To truly love . . . is to tear down walls.*

After some thought, I realized how spiritual this concept of hurt and safety really is. After all. Who loves me more than God? Who keeps me safer than God? Who do I hurt more than God? And it isn't just me.

Some say that love and respect are the keys to a vibrant marriage. But what if a couple has love and respect for each other but still struggles with trust and safety? To truly love with the purest of loves, an agape love, is to tear down all the walls, backfill the moat, and fling the windows and doors open wide.

It trusts that the action of love and respect is a safety that will stand guard against all comers. The amount of vulnerability living in the "house that is you" becomes apparent, as does your ability to give the power, the keys to every door, to only one person, who in turn gives you the keys to their house, too.

You love and hold each other in high esteem, but do you feel safe with them? Do you feel the safety in a marriage that allows you to accept the peace God wants for you?

— KIM LANIER

Food for Thought

Marriage is a lifelong commitment. But we often treat it as a sentence, as in prison. How? We don't make ourselves entirely vulnerable to our spouse. We ignore our fundamental needs for safety and protection because we fear they won't be able to fulfill that necessity. Or they won't provide it in the way we expect.

Like Maslow's hierarchy, we cannot receive other essentials in our marriage if the basic foundation of trust and safety is missing. A relationship cannot survive in the absence of trust. Doubt and fear will overshadow confidence and reliance, two critical ingredients in a successful marriage.

The Bible says that the Holy Spirit searches all things within our hearts. Ask the Lord to reveal any area(s) where you lack trust or faith in your mate. Express your feelings to them lovingly and secure their assistance in resolving the issue (i.e., give them permission). Invest yourself 100% in seeking to regain and rebuild the hope that you once had.

PRAYER, PATIENCE, AND PRAISE

THE RECIPE for true success in our Christian faith involves three simple yet powerful ingredients—prayer, patience, and praise. Let's explore each.

PRAYER

I Thessalonians 5:17 tells us to "pray without ceasing." And in the garden, Jesus prayed, "My Father, if it be possible, let this cup pass from me; nevertheless, not as I will, but as you will." And a second time, Jesus prayed, "My Father, if this cannot pass until I drink it, your will be done."

There have been many things in our marriage that we had no control over. Because as human beings, we are helpless to solve our situation, but we can *always* pray. With all three of my children and my wife, I have faced times when their lives were out of my control and out of the doctor's hands. I could only turn to the One in control, the One who knew the master plan: God.

So, I began to pray for health, healing, and a miracle. As I prayed, the Lord spoke to me and asked, "Whose child is this? Who gave this child to you? Do you think I will forsake them?" Just as Hannah had given Samuel to the Lord, I had also dedicated my children to the Lord, and it was time to let them go, for they were gifts that the Lord had loaned us.

This is when I realized I needed to pray the same prayer that Jesus prayed that night when he was grieved in the garden, "Your will be done." From that moment on, my prayer was for me, not my children or spouse, but for me! It was for the faith to trust in the Lord's plan, for the strength to accept his will, and for the peace that passes all understanding by knowing, "your will be done."

PATIENCE

The Psalmist wrote in chapter 37, verse 7, "Be still before the Lord and wait patiently for him." In times of trial or testing, I have to wait, to be patient, for however long it takes.

When Joseph's brothers threw him into the pit, he prayed and then patiently waited to be sold into slavery. He continued to wait after being thrown into prison for many years. And finally, Joseph was not only released into freedom but into a position to save his family.

All blessings come in the Lord's time, and just as He revealed to Joseph that he must be still before the Lord and wait patiently, so must we. Be patient with your spouse, your children, and yourself. I don't know what the future holds, but I know the Lord holds the future, and He is patiently waiting for me to get there.

PRAISE

Ephesians 5:20 tells us to "give praise at all times for all things in the name of our Lord Jesus Christ, to God, even the Father." Joseph, Daniel, and his friends praised the Lord in everything they did. Even if it meant they would be thrown into prison, a fiery furnace, or into a pit of hungry lions. Their actions planted a seed of praise into the hearts and minds of those watching them.

Late one night, I sat in the ICU, praying and praising the Lord for what He had done. Years later, the nurse who had been on duty at that time told one of my family members what she remembered about a particular situation:

> She had come to tell me I had to leave because we were not allowed to sleep there. As she got closer, she noticed my open bible, saw my lips moving, tears running down my cheeks, and realized I was praying over my son, giving thanks for the success of his surgery.

Seeds were planted that night. Praise the Lord with your thoughts, words, and actions, knowing that you are planting seeds of praise and salvation. Seeds that will be watered, cultivated, and harvested by someone else. But the harvest will only come if seeds are planted.

Talk to God as if He is sitting next to you because He is! Be still and wait for His answer because He is listening. And give thanks and praise Him in all you do, and He will give you the desires of your heart.

—BOBBY MANTHEI

Food for Thought

A kingdom of God principle involves the planting seeds of faith. When a farmer has no crops, he goes out and plants seeds. Nothing will happen without that process. Likewise, nothing will happen in our lives if we don't plant some seeds.

Every living thing on the earth began as a seed. Your relationship (which is ALIVE) started with a seed.

In the space below, list what you need more of in your life (i.e., the *produce*). Next to them, write the seeds you need to plant that will result in that produce. Finally, use the three "P's" to grow your faith and reap a harvest, spiritually and physically.

THE PRODUCE	THE SEED
e.g., Money	Giving to others (Read Luke 6:38)
Wisdom	Daily Bible reading

_____ _____

_____ _____

_____ _____

_____ _____

_____ _____

_____ _____

_____ _____

THE PUZZLE

ARE YOU SOMEONE who enjoys putting puzzles together? I (Scott) am not because I don't have the patience for it. Pieces don't fit, and I get frustrated trying piece after piece to make them fit.

However, my wife, Lori, loves puzzles. In 2004, we went on a Spring Break vacation with our friends Sherman & Tammy Aten and their kids to Ruidoso, New Mexico. Lori and Tammy put together a beautiful puzzle that took them hours over a couple of days, but finally, they completed it.

Life is a lot like a puzzle. You can't see the complete picture until all the pieces are together. Sometimes, things don't seem to fit or make sense. It can frustrate, and you may even feel like giving up. On February 8th, 2007, God gave me a piece of a puzzle. During my morning quiet time, He gave me a verse:

God, who has called you into fellowship with his
Son, Jesus Christ our Lord, is faithful.
1 Corinthians 1:9 NCV

God nudged me and told me he was faithful, which I logged in my journal. He then drilled that truth into me for an entire year. I didn't understand what was happening until March 2nd, 2008, standing at the accident scene of our three girls on their way to

SHERMAN & TAMMY ATEN

church. Our oldest daughter, Jennifer, had been taken by helicopter to the hospital. And our youngest daughter, Brianna, was taken by ambulance. Both sustained serious injuries, but they would be "okay." However, our middle daughter, Alyssa, died in the accident.

When given the news that Alyssa had gone to be with the Lord, it was as if I stood outside my body watching everything. I was numb; time had stopped. At that moment, a lighted billboard flashed in my mind with 1 Corinthians 1:9. The Lord told me, "Trust me. I am faithful." And I immediately knew he had prepared me over an entire year for this very moment.

Suddenly, like puzzle pieces coming together, the picture became clear. The Lord impressed on me standing there to look to my left; I did, and it was looking at the past. He clarified why he wanted me to have one-on-one time with Alyssa. And why He had instructed me to write her a five-page letter expressing my love and pride for her just a few days earlier. He knew I needed to say it all so I wouldn't beat myself up afterward, wishing I would have said something. God showed me He is faithful in the past.

Then, He impressed me to view the present. God saw to every detail. The man who gave us the news about Alyssa was a good friend and fellow brother in Christ; his wife would be the nurse who worked on my daughter Brianna at the hospital. Many of the first responders were close friends and fellow church members. Our best friends were there

God saw to every detail.

with us. A nurse, who had been through a similar event as a child, prayed with Jennifer as she got off the helicopter at the hospital. God laid it on one man's heart to pay for the funeral. He saw to every detail and showed me He is faithful in the present.

We found Alyssa's journal after the accident, where she poured her heart out to the Lord, expressing her love for him and her willingness to be used by Him. She wanted to lead people to Christ and to help bring unity and transformation to our community. Her visitation was a six-hour continuous flow of people where we could share Christ with hundreds of people one-on-one. Her dream had been to pack our new sanctuary, and her funeral was filled to overflowing with friends and loved ones.

About a month after the accident, I was asked to share a devotional at our church deacon's meeting. I prayed to the Lord for an hour, asking Him what He wanted me to share. He gave me seven things that I wrote down. But the last two were "pieces of a puzzle . . . tell how they fit . . . Lori and Tammy's puzzle" and "show them the puzzle." I immediately knew I was to get the puzzle that Lori and Tammy had assembled from that trip in 2004. However, I didn't even know if we had it. I didn't even remember the puzzle's theme, just that it was in a blue box.

On the top shelf of the closet outside Alyssa's room was a blue box. I fell to my knees and cried like a baby when I saw what the puzzle was. The puzzle was Jesus standing in Heaven with someone who had just died. He had His arms wrapped around them, and the puzzle title was "Home At Last." God told me to show them that puzzle and tell them that he is a God faithful in the past, present, and future!

My daughter's prayers were heard and answered by God. Since her death, many people have come to Christ, and believers have been strengthened through her story, testimony, and journal entries. The Lord readied our family to travel to various countries and share about a faithful God who wants a relationship with us.

This is all part of a giant puzzle He is continually adding pieces to. And each piece brings the picture into ever-increasing clarity.

Does your life seem like a puzzle you can't figure out? God is using everything in your life for a purpose as part of His greater plan. I assure you He is faithful and wants you to experience His faithfulness. At the accident scene, I told God, "I will trust you as you are faithful." I'm so glad I did; the puzzle became very clear!

—SCOTT & LORI DIX

Food for Thought

1. Do you sometimes feel you know about God but haven't "Experienced God?" Ask him to reveal himself to you. Ref. John 14:21.

2. Do you believe God has a purpose and plan for you, your marriage, and your family? Spend time looking back at the past and the present and ask God to clarify what he's doing in your life. Reference Ephesians 2:10, Philippians 1:6, Acts 9:15, Jeremiah 1:5, Job 1 & 2 and 38-42.

3. Describe your trust level with God. Is it based on your circumstances? Actions follow beliefs, so what do your actions say? Reference Proverbs 3:5-6.

Father, thank you for being a faithful God and having a plan and purpose for my life. Please help me always seek you and make it my aim to please you; I want to experience you. Have your way in me and in my marriage and family. In Jesus' name. Amen.

REFLUX

> *Awake, O sleeper, and arise from the dead and*
> *Christ will shine upon you and give you light. Look*
> *carefully then how you walk! Live purposefully and*
> *worthy and accurately, not as the unwise, making*
> *most of the time, because the days are evil.*
> Ephesians 5:14-15 AMPC

BREATHE DEEP. Take a breath in. Take a breath out. Try blowing bubbles in a cup of water through this special straw. Count slowly to ten in a breathy voice (i.e., Marilyn Monroe style). That's what my doctor, an otolaryngologist (*Sorry, that's the word. Use your vowels!*) from UT Medical Center in Dallas, told me. Yep, I know. It sounds like Elisha saying, "Go and dip in the Jordan seven times, Naaman. And you will be well." Silent acid reflux was damaging my vocal cords at night while I was sleeping. And I didn't even know it!

The key word here is "silent." I had no usual physical symptoms. No heartburn or waking up choking or coughing. After my scope, taken at Baylor in Ft. Worth, the pictures of my cords were purple & so inflamed it looked like I had *four* vocal cords! Normal people only have two light pink vocal cords.

Wow! My body was trying to put me out of commission by burning my cords, and I didn't even know it. Since I sing & speak for a living—well, let's just say that's not good!

During the nine-month process of dealing with this situation and healing, I had to be re-trained in how to speak & sing *without* tension. Because I had been overcompensating for so long, my larynx muscles had learned some terrible habits. If I hadn't been a singer, I probably wouldn't have known what was going on until severe damage had been done. I could talk fine, but when I tried to sing, that's when I knew something wasn't right.

Be aware that there are some "incognito" acids having a party while we sleep. We're out like a light and clueless about the damage being done because of the poor choices we've made.

There's a lesson regarding marriage in this, as well. When we become oblivious to the subtle harm eroding our relationship, it can cause harm without us even knowing it.

I'm not a doctor with a title that is 12 letters long. But I know this: Before we face irreparable damage, be wise and take inventory with each other on a weekly basis. Have a specific time when you can connect. Breathe in and breathe out through the daily challenges—together! Touch base often and communicate.

Most importantly, pray, pray, pray. Otherwise, you may need to spend over nine months repairing the three-cord strand that is your connection. And I can't tell you how much that will cost. But it could come at a great expense.

—SHERMAN ATEN

Food for Thought

Like the hidden damage acid can do to your vocal cords, there are unnoticed factors that can harm your marriage. Review the list below and plan to correct behaviors that have the potential to hurt your relationship.

- Your friends are more important to you than your spouse.
- You don't regularly attend a corporate Christian gathering together for spiritual training and growth.
- You don't share common interests.
- You take for granted that you "know" your spouse's likes and dislikes.
- You stop pursuing your spouse like you did when you were dating.
- You have let your personal appearance slide.
- You view your marriage as a contract rather than as a partnership.

SHE'S THE ONE

I DON'T KNOW if you believe your spouse is the "one." But I hope you do. Living with that belief will help you explain and accept many things. It will also help remove the word "divorce" from your vocabulary.

However, if you've already been there and done that, no worries—God has a way. This applies to your marriage relationship today. Because where you are now in your marriage is the genuine concern. And what you believe about God's sovereign will and your free choices will color your perspective.

I love what Charles Spurgeon, a prominent English preacher of the 19th century, said about reconciling the apparent tension in the Bible between God's sovereignty and man's free will. He said:

> **I never have to reconcile friends.**
> **Divine sovereignty and human responsibility**
> **have never had a falling out with each other.**
> **I do not need to reconcile**
> **what God has joined together.**

It's difficult even to describe the numerous ways the woman God created for me in Tammy Payne and I fit together. Do you know how Eve was crafted just for Adam? Well, that's what I mean about Tammy and me. She was literally taken from a rib in his side and created specifically for him.

Why can't it be that way for us? I know we all think we had something to do with choosing a spouse. But there's no way I was smart enough to pick her out of every other female in the universe and win her heart—by myself. I had to have had help.

In Ephesians 5, Paul says that marriage is a mystery. *Hmm,* I wonder. Is God sovereign, even over my choice of a spouse? Marriage is the most holy and meant-to-be permanent transaction I will make with another human being while on this planet. Are we left all to our own on this?

Tammy and I started our relationship as best friends. *And I highly recommend that beginning to every couple!* I did have to engage the "all is fair in love and war" mentality just a bit to win her over. But I did it by passing a note, just as I did in fourth grade to my first-ever crush. Back in grade school, I was so infatuated but scared to speak to her. So, I did what any nine-year-old boy would do; I wrote her a note and had my friends pass it up. The note read, "Will you go with me? Yes or No." Whew! She circled "Yes" and then passed the message back to me. Of course, we broke up the next day! But for that one day, success!

> **Her reply was, "You have the power to change that."**

That's not exactly the note I wrote and passed to Tammy at age 21 while sitting several rows behind her on the WBU International Choir bus. At the time, she was in a relationship with a friend. Actually, with my best friend. We were all best friends. We hadn't discovered that *two's company, three's a crowd.*

So, in fourth-grade style, I wrote a note saying I always thought and felt that if any two of the three of us were to be together, it was her and me. And that's all she needed.

Her reply was, "You have the power to change that."

Done. Success once again. But thank God this one lasted for more than a day!

The beauty of marriage is that there is another soul who is made to know you in every way. To know you, and to KNOW you. One who is perfectly equipped to handle your pluses and your minuses—God's genius idea!

No, things aren't always as pretty as this may sound, but anything worth something requires effort. And don't be fooled. Just because you both attend church, have religion, or practice Christianity doesn't guarantee your marriage will be good. You are both responsible for that.

So, will it help to know this person is the one God made for you? It helps me to live in the mystery, even if it sounds "fairytale-ish," that the woman I'm married to is the one God planned to be *my* wife. I choose to believe that. And I know SHE'S THE ONE!

Making known to us the mystery (secret) of His will of
His plan, of His purpose. In accordance with His good
pleasure which He previously purposed and set forth
in Him. And we were also chosen and appointed
beforehand in accordance with His purpose,
Who works out everything in agreement
with His design and will.
Ephesians 1: 9, 11 AMPC

—SHERMAN ATEN

Food for Thought

In Genesis, the Bible teaches that Adam and Eve were suitable counterparts for each other. In other words, what Adam lacked, Eve provided, and vice versa.

Knowing God designed your spouse to balance you brings confidence and assurance in your relationship. You don't have to be twins, agreeing on and liking the same things. Instead, your life is balanced by the other, keeping you on an even keel.

List a couple of personality distinctions between you and your spouse below. How have these differences proven to be what you needed to become a better individual or a successful couple?

He is:_____

She is:_____

But together, we are:

_____

He is:_____

She is:_____

But together, we are:

_____

He is:_____

She is:_____

But together, we are:

_____

He is:_____

She is:_____

But together, we are:

_____

He is:_____

She is:_____

But together, we are:

_____

SHOWING UP

I AM BEYOND excited to spend the day with my granddaughter, Maren. As I drive up to her house, I see a new black Jeep at the top of the hill. My first thought is, *I wonder when they bought the Jeep?*

Then I realize it might not be their Jeep because it is definitely not their driveway. I had turned in one driveway too soon. Shifting into reverse, I back straight down the driveway. But I didn't check my review mirrors or look at the backup camera!

Quickly, it becomes apparent that I am no longer backing down a driveway. This driveway curves just a little down the hill, and unfortunately, I did not follow that curve! As a result, my car is sliding down the hill with squares of freshly laid sod attached under the tires, gathering more sod squares the further it goes.

The sliding stops abruptly as the car hits large rocks at the bottom of the hill. I am mortified. I have demolished the Mayor Pro Tem's beautifully landscaped yard in seconds!

After several futile attempts, it is evident that I will not be driving my front-wheel drive vehicle out of this ripped-up sod, backed with several inches of fertile black soil. The rain had been pouring off and on for three days. And the fertile black soil is now "slicker than mucus" mud. Perfect for sod, but not so good for gaining traction.

Immediately, I did what I do when finding myself in a hopeless situation—call my husband, Bobby. And he did what he does— quickly showed up to help. When my husband arrives, I listen intently to his instructions, thinking *I am so eager to help him get me out of this mess.*

The first attempt at pulling me out is tough-going. We make a few inches of progress before *his* back tires start spinning fast but going nowhere. I am smart enough to know this isn't good. Quickly shifting into "Park," I put the emergency brake on to protect our progress, waiting for further instruction. A kind neighbor stops to help, so he and Bobby discuss the unique situation.

> *I am smart enough to know this isn't good.*

Then, my sweet husband walks around to the passenger window to talk to me. But in my heart, I felt he wasn't talking to me in the same tone he was talking to the neighbor. So I say, "Fine, the neighbor can drive!" Bobby turns and walks back up to the pickup while I head next door.

The next sound I hear is the heavy chain jolting his pickup to a halt, with his back tires screeching on the concrete driveway. Running back, I see my sweet Bobby getting out of his pickup and heading toward my Explorer. I watch as Bobby realizes no one is in the driver's seat!

At about the same time, he glances up and sees me. He looks back at the car, and then he looks back at me. I forgot to tell you, my husband reads lips a lot. He can understand almost everything you say if you look at him when you talk. However, he did not hear me say I was going to the house. My sweet husband is giving his all to get me out of *my* predicament. But not only have I put the car in park with the emergency brake on, I have completely bailed!

Fortunately, at that moment, another friendly neighbor with a big four-wheel drive pickup stops and offers to help. Effortlessly he pulls my vehicle out of the slick muddy sod, and we thank the nice neighbor. I also apologize profusely to the Mayor Pro Tem and his family for the damage I caused and compensate them for the cost. We washed my car the next day, and you would never know anything had happened. But of course, *I* knew something had happened.

Bobby had lovingly shown up for me—again. As a result, I adore and appreciate my husband even more today than I did yesterday, though I didn't think that was possible. My love for him is a little sweeter, and my respect is more profound, which also didn't seem likely.

God also lovingly showed up for me again. He literally pulled me out of another rock-bottom mess. Yet I do the same thing to God as with my husband; I get distracted. Then, I justify and make excuses for my actions, instantly reacting rather than seeking His guidance.

After digging myself so deep and finally hitting rock bottom, I call Him for help. When He shows up, I listen intently for a while. *I am so eager to help Him get me out of this mess!* That is until things don't go as perfectly as I prefer.

Then I shift into park and set the emergency brake. I have even been known to physically, mentally, and emotionally bail on my God, my Lord, and Savior!

God, forgive me. I am so sorry. I love you. I love you even more than I did yesterday.

Always remember: God loves you. He forgives you. He is waiting for that call for help. All we have to do is release the emergency brake and show up. Show up with a willing servant's heart. God will do the rest.

—MARGIE MANTHEI

Food for Thought

Independence is a mixed bag. We want to be individual thinkers who choose our beliefs and make wise decisions based on experience. But in a relationship, being too independent can become a problem.

Scientific studies show that independence impacts both communication (*or lack thereof*) and your partner's self-esteem. Often, a spouse feels rejected when we don't accept their care or assistance.

It is healthy to depend on your mate and even become vulnerable when assistance is needed. This is commonly referred to as *interdependence*, a process of collaboration and connection with each other. Through interdependency, your marriage has a YOU, a ME, and an US. It is being mindful of who we are and who we are not.

Spend time with your spouse, discussing ways to show up for them through interdependence. What are situations where you can work as a team to accomplish success in your marriage?

SIX WORDS

I ENJOY the concept of the six-word story or memoir. The idea is that brevity of words is a virtue. Short stories consisting of just six words, inspired by Ernest Hemingway's famous challenge and first six-word story, "For sale: baby shoes, never worn."

The Bible speaks of marriage. Some verses can be expressed in six words.

Humility, gentleness, patience - bearing one another.

Ephesians 4:2-3

I'm a seal upon your heart.

Song of Solomon 8:6

Honor, devotion - one another above yourselves.

Romans 12:10

I am going to try a few short six-word stories.

- ✓ "Yes, dear. I know, dear. Whatever."
- ✓ "Your mother is staying how long?"
- ✓ "I love you. What's for dinner."

In marriage, sometimes, the fewer words that are spoken, the better. Sometimes, after too many words, even just six - silence follows.

More often than not, a lack of words will silence a marriage. A lack of action will silence the words. However, there is something to be said for the brevity of words; you cannot listen while you are talking.

The first prayers and the first marriage—which came first? I think in its purest form, probably prayer. Regardless, the communication between spouses and God should be very similar. We are supposed to be having a dialogue, not a monologue. The listening is just as important as the talking.

Trying to ensure a measured response is better than using the phrase, "I didn't mean it like that." Practicing communicating with one may help communicating with the other.

Actually, I have heard from some couples that praying together to God is the best communication they have ever had between each other. God the counselor, healer, advisor, and forgiver. Not a bad idea!

The next time you find yourself rehearsing a speech for the spouse, maybe just find the right six words. Oh, and I thought of one more six-word story:

For God so loved, He gave . . .
John 3:16

—KIM LANIER

Food for Thought

Let's make this week's devotional "food" something fun! Using the blanks below, write three six-word phrases or stories expressing your love for the other. Be creative, kind, and enjoy!

_____ _____ _____ _____ _____ _____.

_____ _____ _____ _____ _____ _____.

_____ _____ _____ _____ _____ _____.

_____ _____ _____ _____ _____ _____.

_____ _____ _____ _____ _____ _____.

_____ _____ _____ _____ _____ _____.

SLEEPLESS NIGHTS

A Few Thoughts on Raising a Child Safely into Adulthood:

Newborn smell . . . sweet . . . cuddly
Will I *ever* sleep again?
Poopy diaper . . . hand to Sherman . . . crying . . . shower
Pray and breathe life on them and God's Word!

BLINK

A toddler running around challenging everything.
Alphabet Numbers leading to read . . . potty training
Pray and breathe life on them and God's Word!

BLINK

Driving them all over to every practice
From baseball, swimming, dance, piano, basketball, football, and
on and on . . . sleepovers
Pray and breathe life on them and God's Word!

BLINK
Now, *they* drive all over to high school activities.
Crushes . . . dates . . . Proms . . . Graduation
Pray and breathe life on them and God's Word!
BLINK

College . . . set their dorm room up . . .
Drive home, crying all the way . . .
Let them choose on some hard things.
Pray and breathe life on them and God's Word!

BLINK

Being a Mom is one of the most rewarding jobs.
It brings some of the greatest joys you will ever have.
It brings some of the greatest pain you will ever experience.

What a unique kind of love is the love of a Mother.
A sacrificial love unlike any other.
Love "BIG" on your Mom today
And say, "Thank You!"

In whichever stage you are in, the Bible says:

**The manna is new every morning
And in just the right proportion we need.**

Grace is also new every morning.
And the Bible says it never runs out.

That's encouraging, isn't it, Mommas?
God has our back.
Remember, too:

The greatest testimony is your salvation.
But the second greatest is the legacy
You leave on those children . . . and grandchildren . . . and great grandchildren.

Pray.
Breathe life.
Model God's Word.

—TAMMY ATEN

Food for Thought

Someone once said, "If it weren't for your Mom, you wouldn't be breathing right now!" Besides the apparent reason, the invaluable worth of mothers is often underestimated. Pope Francis said, "A world without mothers would be inhumane . . . lacking tenderness."

Motherhood comes with a job description that no one could fill and with a pauper's pay. But it's also a parent's most important role in a child's life.

Write down five (5) qualities you think are essential as a parent to demonstrate in your home. Consider the sacrificial love of the two mothers who came to King Solomon claiming that a baby was theirs. (See 1 Kings 3:16-28).

1. _____

2. _____

3. _____

4. _____

5. _____

Who are the most influential mothers in your life? Have you thanked them recently? If not, give them a call or send a note of appreciation.

STOP THE COMPARISONS

MY WIFE is absolutely beautiful inside and out. But you'd never know it when you ask her. Much of it is because of a trait many women struggle with: women compare everything.

It breeds massive insecurity because you never measure up. The result is enormous pressure to be enough, do enough, and work enough to measure up. You never do. It's the lie Satan inserted in the Garden of Eden: You are *not enough*.

It's much better to be like God. When I compare myself to the person next to me, I can never be who God created me to be. The byproduct is an identity built on activity, beauty, capacity, or tenacity with enormous pressure to become what we are not.

When they measure themselves with themselves and compare themselves with one another, they are without understanding and behave unwisely.

2 Corinthians 10:12 AMP

Women struggle with depression much more than their male counterparts because they compare God-given beauty to silicone and plastic images of celebrities rather than articulating the creativity God unleashes in them. Comparison not only makes you harder on yourself, but it also tells God He didn't do a good enough job. The message is reinforced: *not enough*.

And if the constant comparing of popularity, beauty, or competence isn't enough, there's always a slew of other things you can throw into the comparison slaw:

- ✓ The accumulation wars.
- ✓ The activity wars.
- ✓ The Mommy Wars.

Why do you think Lori Loughlin created fake athletic profiles and paid $500,000 to get her two daughters into USC? Aunt Becky's take was she only did what any Mom would do to get her daughters into a prestigious university if they had the means. We compare our spouses and marriages, our homes or vacations—everything ad infinitum.

What's the worst possible thing you can do with those who struggle with comparisons? Give them a phone with a great camera to post on social media. It leads to dark, dark places because comparison is essentially competition for approval and acceptance and identity that leads to a veneer, a façade, a faux identity rooted in false bravado, insecurity, and inauthenticity.

So, how can husbands help their wives when they compare themselves with others? Be a reminder of how absolutely fabulous your wife is. Remind her she is becoming the "me" that God created her to be. Don't just mouth the words; mean them! She is fearfully and wonderfully made.

—DR. JOE STEWART

Food for Thought

When they measure themselves with themselves and compare themselves with one another, they are without understanding and behave unwisely.
1 Corinthians 10:12 AMP

Take some time on a date night or a weekly check-in to talk about where you struggle with insecurity. Where do you feel like you are "not enough"? Use this time as well to use the following statements.

- I am enough because the Scriptures say _____.
- Satan's lie underlying my feelings of insecurity is _____.
- Spend some time as a spouse highlighting each other's strengths.

Dave and Ann Wilson use the idea of luggage as the burdens we carry. Husbands tend to carry one suitcase at a time. Wives are often juggling multiple suitcases. This leads to feelings of insecurity in a variety of areas (parenting, tasks, chores, intimacy, work, etc.). Talk about the loads you are carrying. How can you help each other lighten these loads?

Then, negotiate a few boundaries for each of your social media and phone habits. Boundaries are personal rules to keep you from personal damage.

- Do we need to set some boundaries for digital sabbaths?
- When are times or areas that are screen-free spaces?
- How should we handle notifications during dates or vacations?

TEN WAYS TO STAY CLOSE FOR A LIFETIME

By wisdom, a house is built, and through
understanding, it is established;
Through knowledge, its rooms are filled
with rare and beautiful treasures.

Proverbs 24:3-4 NIV

WISDOM and knowledge come through the repetition of good habits. These ten pieces of advice can help you build a lifetime of intimacy with your spouse:

1. Continue to say, "I love you." After all, God reminds us of this in Jeremiah 31:3, "I have loved you with an everlasting love; I have drawn you with loving-kindness."
2. Maintain your sense of humor. Be able to laugh at yourself, but never make jokes at your spouse's expense. Proverbs 17:22 says, "A cheerful heart is a good medicine, but a crushed spirit dries up the bones."
3. Pray together regularly as a couple. More than just the blessing over a meal, spending time together seeking intimacy with the Lord builds greater intimacy between a husband and wife.

Do not be anxious about anything,
but in everything, by prayer and petition,
with thanksgiving, present your requests to God.
And the peace of God,
which transcends all understanding,
will guard your hearts and minds in Christ Jesus.
Philippians 4:6-7

---

4. Hold hands and hug. Physical touch communicates being connected on many levels. "But Esau ran to meet Jacob and embraced him; he threw his arms around his neck and kissed him. And they wept." (Genesis 33:4)

5. Truly listen to each other. Give eye contact and undivided attention to hear what your mate says. James 1:19 says, "My dear brothers, take note of this: Everyone should be quick to listen, slow to speak, and slow to become angry."

6. Express appreciation and give compliments to each other. Sometimes, we're more considerate and polite with co-workers and strangers than with the one who is more special to us than anyone else. "Therefore, encourage one another and build each other up." (1 Thessalonians 5:11)

7. Plan a couple's getaway. It can be just a day or two or longer, but getting away occasionally without the kids or other distractions helps keep the focus on your marriage and can keep those fires burning. "Come, my lover, let us go to the countryside; let us spend the night in the villages." (Song of Songs 7:11—*Did Solomon and his bride find an Airbnb?*)

8. Study the Bible and worship together. Tell each other what the Lord may be teaching you from His Word. Hebrews 10:24-25 says, "Let us think of ways to motivate one another

to acts of love and good works. And let us not neglect our meeting together, as some people do, but encourage one another."

9. Reminisce about the past and dream about the future. Pull out a photo album and talk about adventures you have taken in the past. Share your dreams for the future.

I thank my God every time I remember you.
Philippians 1:3

---

10. "Above all, clothe yourselves with love, which binds us all together in perfect harmony," as taught in Colossians 3:14.

—ED AND ELIZABETH PLANTS

Food for Thought

Over the next few weeks, try implementing two or three of the ideas expressed in this teaching. Select them in advance, then make a specific plan to implement them into your daily interactions.

In a month or so, reflect on the changes you've made. Is there a difference in the quality of your communication and day-to-day living? Consider the questions below:

- What are some loving habits we have neglected?
- Do we hold and hug each other?
- Do we laugh with each other (not at each other)?
- Do we maintain eye contact and give our undivided attention when sharing?
- How often do we offer compliments and appreciation to our spouse?
- When was the last time we got away—just the two of us—without distractions or interruptions?
- Are we studying God's word together?
- Do we dream?
- Do we reminisce?
- Have I told my spouse that I love them today?

THROUGH THE EYES OF A CHILD

SLOWLY AS I WENT down into the glistening water, I sang in my mind, "*How great is our God. Sing with me. How great is our God. And all will see. How great, how great is our God.*"

Coming out of the baptistery, the preacher said, "Alyssa Diane Dix is baptized in the name of the Father, the Son, and the Holy Spirit." Again, while he prayed, I stood there contemplating this song. After all I'd gone through, I'd known how great he was. I thought back to the various things He had done that had changed my life.

. . . .

Leaning heavily against the large expanse of the tall white bathroom wall, outlined in little dull-colored flowers, I stood, somehow comforted by its bigness. My older sister, Jennifer, and I brushed our teeth while my little sister fell asleep. Silently brushing away my tears, I listened attentively to the coming argument.

Then I sat, hearing the sickening, strained silence, except for the clink and clang of my mom cleaning the kitchen and my un-calmed pounding heart beating loudly. Everything went utterly still, and then I heard the repeated hushing of secret whispers of an ongoing argument that had gone on for a very long while.

Dreadfully, I inched forward, sliding my little feet across the floor like a person on their way to jail. Until I finally reached the large door, opening it for just a peak—then a bit wider. Everything went quiet. Nervously stepping out, I could see my mom had marks on her face where her tears had gone down.

My parents motioned for me and my sister to come out; they needed to talk to us. When they finally spoke, my life changed. In precious seconds, my whole world as I'd known it rocked. Divorce! *What?*

"It just didn't work," they said. But they were still on friendly terms.

We'd live upstairs at Grama's and Papa's house with Mommy only. Daddy wouldn't live with us, but we'd see Daddy, and he reassured us that he would always love us.

He got an apartment in Ft. Worth, and we saw him every other weekend, on Tuesdays and Thursdays, and a few special holidays. But no matter what they said or did to reassure us, everything had changed, and Daddy still wouldn't be there.

I was a princess, taken away from her castle. Nothing would ever be the same, and that made me scared. So sometimes, by myself, I'd sit down, hug my legs against me, and wish everything could be as it once was. I knew it probably wouldn't happen, but that didn't stop me from hoping and praying to God for help.

As time passed, I began to adjust to my new life, one without a dad to come home to. My dad came on Tuesdays and Thursdays to take us out to eat. We took turns picking different places; we loved our favorite, Pizza Inn. Afterward, he'd usually take us to the park or sometimes to the bowling alley or the Gulch to play miniature golf.

And on weekends, when we went to Ft. Worth, we'd go to Chuckie Cheese with my dad's best friend and his family, Discovery Zone, or Kid's Playhouse.

Then, nearly a year and a half later, my dad decided to marry again to a lady he worked with. We weren't pleased because she'd never be our mom, but we thought my dad was happy. My dad moved into her house, so we had to go there on the weekends that he had us.

At first, we got along okay. But after a little while, we didn't like going there. Even though we did cool things and got to be around Daddy, we didn't like her. She played favorites, and her house was dark and scary. It seemed that the walls jumped out at you or closed you in. Although we preferred to stay home, we continued our visits.

A year later, my dad took us home one night after eating out and said he'd like to talk to Mommy. That wasn't an unusual request since they'd stayed on friendly terms. So, they went outside to sit and talk in my dad's old hail-damaged blue Geo Metro while my sisters and I got ready for bed.

An hour later, they both came in looking so happy and told us they needed to talk to us. Of course, that worried us, but they saw our expressions and told us it was a good thing. At a snail's pace, we all entered the living room and sat on the beige carpet across from my mom and dad, who were leaning on each other and holding hands.

What was going on? They took a deep breath, turned to each other, and smiled. Then Dad told us that he was getting divorced from the woman he worked with and that he and Mom were getting back together. Jumping up, we hugged our parents, crying happily, yelling and shouting, all babbling at once, saying what a perfect family, a dream come true. I was a princess coming back home to her castle.

We found out later that my dad had been saved and asked my mom to forgive him for his adultery with the other woman while they were married. Mom told him she had rededicated her life and needed to ask him for his forgiveness. My parents had talked about how it was each their fault and how God had changed them. That's when they discussed getting back together and prayed about it, then came to tell us the God-given news.

My dad moved back in but slept on the couch until he and my mom remarried. He then talked to our preacher about becoming a church member, where we all went. They had changed and now put God first in everything they did. We'd always been loved. But it seemed we were loved more deeply and unconditionally. They were both very peaceful and happy and had truly changed.

They had changed and now put God first in everything they did.

On March 12th, while we dressed, my mom fixed our hair and gave us a small gold locket. I was blissfully happy as I walked down the aisle as a bridesmaid, along with my little sister, Brianna, the flower girl. My sister, Jennifer, came in right before my mom as the maid of honor; then my mom entered last.

Mom was so radiant she glowed like the sun. Even the tears she cried didn't make a difference. She was beautiful. We all stood there watching her like firecrackers ready to explode.

After the wedding, my sister and I began to ask questions about receiving God as our Savior. We wanted to know why—besides the apparent facts—my parents always praised him. We learned more through parents, Sunday School, and others, and then we accepted him. We talked to my preacher more about God's abounding love and how Christ died for us, and we set a date to be baptized.

. . . .

While standing there in waist-deep in the water, I thought about my favorite bible verse:

> *"For I know the plans I have for you," declares the Lord, "plans to prosper you and not to harm you, plans to give you hope and a future."*
> Jeremiah 29:11 NIV

God didn't plan to hurt me; He actually did things that were better for me, although I couldn't see it then. He is amazing. God brought my family back together, and we all became Christians.

What more could I ever want or need than the love and mercy of Jesus Christ? Now I know the incomparable love of Christ, and I was changed forever through divorce, even though God had a plan. Having grown spiritually since then, Christ now colors everything I say or do. Where would I be without him?

NOTE: My daughter, Alyssa Dix, wrote these words a few months before she passed away in a car accident on March 2, 2008, while on her way to church. She lived a full life even though she had just turned sixteen a few days earlier. These words display her faith in her Sovereign Lord, who has a plan for each of us and for our marriage and family.

—SCOTT DIX

Food for Thought

Sometimes, we don't see God's hand in a difficult situation. We aren't on the other side and only see the mountain before us. But God is working behind the scenes to draw us to Himself.

- What is your view of God? Describe His attributes in very intimate detail.
- What do you think is His view of you? Describe this explicitly.
- What are the most difficult trials or tribulations you have experienced?
- Did you see or experience God in them?
- How did it affect your view of Him?

Father, I praise you that you are a Sovereign God; nothing escapes your notice, including me and everything that happens to me. I want to draw closer to you and better understand and live out the plan and purpose for my life per your will and desire as you created me. Please help me experience You. In Jesus' name. Amen.

TO THOSE MEN
(SETTLING DOWN THOSE SPAGHETTI NOODLES)

FOR WHAT IT'S WORTH, men, I'm just offering my two cents of advice. But men primarily function in boxes. Like a waffle—one box, one subject at a time. Women are more like spaghetti. One noodle touches another noodle and then off to another thought or matter.

So, men, if you can help settle down our noodles a little in the bedroom, it might be more productive for you. LOL. (*Just saying!*)

As women, we can't shut down as easily as men. She's still buying groceries, folding laundry, working, and making kids lunches. Oh, and what about the plan for homework, football practice, or the drop-off at dance lessons floating around in her head?

So . . . maybe a "setup" for her will help. Here are a few ideas on a woman's ideal setup:

- ✓ A glass of wine (or a Coke Zero for me),
- ✓ A bubble bath that you ran for her,
- ✓ A candlelit backdrop,
- ✓ Music playing softly,
- ✓ A favorite new fiction book, or

✓ A new magazine, and best of all
✓ One hour ALONE!

You'll be amazed at what these simple actions will settle down or shake off for her. And the night might still be miraculously young! *Wink, wink*

But you say, "My wife doesn't want all that?" Then, figure out what she *does* want and put it into place.

—TAMMY ATEN

I will praise You,
for I am fearfully and wonderfully made:
marvelous are Your works;
and that my soul knows well.

Psalm 139:14 NKJV

Food for Thought

How are you and your spouse different? Do you celebrate those differences? Or allow them to irritate you? If we are exactly the same, then one of us is unnecessary.

Every marriage is a one-of-a-kind creation. It's okay to have differences; that is perfectly normal. The key is how you respond to your spouse's differences.

This week, when you are irritated because your spouse believes or says something different from you, realize they are your perfect complement. Perhaps respond in a counterintuitive way and see things from another perspective.

List ways your partner can set you up for a romantic encounter. Honor these ideas with respect and love rather than seeing them as dissimilar from what you might have expected.

HUSBAND'S IDEAS FOR A ROMANTIC "SETUP":

_____

_____

_____

_____

WIFE'S IDEAS FOR A ROMANTIC "SETUP":

_____

_____

_____

_____

UNDERSTANDING WAYS

NANCY AND I got married when we were nineteen. We had something in common: we were both in love with me! She often says I take a lot for granted. The book of Peter teaches:

Husbands, live with your wives
in an understanding way.
1 Peter 3:7 ESV

The meaning here is that we need to learn to communicate, which is easier said than done.

We raised three daughters, so I was a minority in a sorority. My family always told me, "*We* don't overspend; *you* under-deposit!" The point is we all think and communicate differently because communication is difficult.

The female brain has 15% more blood flow than a male and a ton of lateral highways connecting both sides of her brain. And on those highways, a lot of traffic is continuously zooming in and out. Whereas a man's connecting fiber is a country road in a slow F150 pickup with a cassette tape playing, "*Country Road take me . . . out to the ballgame . . . or out of here!*"

Remember, her mind is like a busy computer with multiple windows open, running simultaneously. And unwanted pop-ups constantly intrude, with little ability to close them out or to ignore the mental or emotional activity until a more convenient time—like when it's not 4th and 1. Because that's how her brain is wired, she naturally experiences and internalizes all thoughts and feelings and then reacts.

It's interrelated in every realm of life. It means what happened in the kitchen this morning affects what happens in the bedroom later.

Men are microwaves; women are slow cookers. Her feelings about what happened with Suzy at the ball game influence her interaction with the life group at church. Telling her, "Just don't think about it," is about as useful as another shovelful of sand in the Sahara. Here's the problem: A man's brain processes deeply, one window at a time. That's it!

A man's brain processes deeply, one window at a time.

So, here's a bit of advice to live with understanding. Listen to your wife without correcting or problem-solving. She's most likely processing, anyway. Gently remind her you are still stuck in first gear when she jumps from one box to another. Plan times for having quality conversations without interruption.

It might mean you are cooking something up for later. But even if that doesn't happen, you are building a friendship—the secret to a thriving marriage.

—DR. JOE STEWART

Food for Thought

Think of a situation where you realized that your brain processes differently than your spouse. Which action did you take to help understand their ways? Here are three ways to understand the unique ways of your spouse:

- Listen without correcting or problem-solving.
- Gently remind them of the differences in which you operate.
- Make a plan to have uninterrupted quality time for conversation.

Try this approach for the next seven days and note the difference it makes in your communication.

A UNITED FRONT

For this reason a man shall leave his father and
mother and be united to his wife,
and the two shall become one flesh.
So they are NO LONGER TWO, but ONE.
Mark 10:7-8 NIV [Emphasis added]

IT'S SOBERING to realize that our **most important decision** to become united for life with someone on this earth doesn't require any training or a certification. Even though an earthly marriage was created to be a Holy thing by God Himself and to serve as a representation of the relationship between the Groom (God's Son, Jesus) and the Bride, His Church.

Goodness—even back in first grade, I was required to take a test to prove I knew how to add two plus two! And yet, nothing is required for an adult to transact a lifelong, legally binding commitment to another adult human being. When we get that pretty parchment license, it states we are now legally married in the eyes of the law and God Himself. Surely, we will have learned something from somebody, somewhere. You bet we have!

Let's start with PARENTING. When did we learn how to do that? And where? We pretty much learned from what took place in our home growing up. We learned what we learned from whoever raised or parented us. And so, we all had different teachers. Which means we do things differently because we are all very different. And that's really a good thing! We are told to embrace our differences. Opposites attract! Thank God we're different in a lot of ways.

When it came to raising our first child, our son, Tammy and I put our different parenting styles out front and center; we had no time to prepare. There was no book written to tell me exactly how to train and discipline this two-year-old, strong-willed, little male angel that God had placed into our home.

And time after time, we faced tests. I don't recommend that anyone do what we did—raising our kids in a 40 ft. RV parked mostly on church parking lots all over the U.S.A. Unless it is God's idea, which, in our case, it was. So, He gave us the grace to do it. And really, it was the most fun ever!

Still, to this day, the scene replays in my head. My wife was a teacher and a musician. And thank God she schooled both of our kids while on the road. So, every day, no matter where we were, school began at 8:00 a.m.

During the day, the principal (me) would be called in because one student had an attitude or something beyond my imagination. *Really, this gift from Heaven said what to his teacher—his mother!?* It leaves you wondering, after you have exhausted every tool of discipline in your portfolio, if anything will work.

And really, it was the most fun ever!

And you've crafted these tools for years by watching other parents "parent" their kids. Perhaps not crafted as well as you could because that was before you had any children. Then you get angry. Forgetting you're a team, you react by issuing a sentence that penalizes all of you.

Or you think you know the best way to handle it. However, you aren't on the "same page" as your spouse. Well, you go ahead & do it according to your way of thinking. Surely the child hasn't a clue that you and mommy don't agree on this.

And you won't always agree. But don't fool yourself. Those little tikes know it and will play you against each other. To this day, even as adults, they know who to call!

All this to say, at the end of the day, consistency and unity win. Your children are a joy of the Lord, the godly fruit of your love for each other. The Lord will use them to mold you, bend you, and sharpen your skills as a mother and father. We were once like them, and yes, we knew how to get whatever from whoever leaned a certain way toward us.

So, confuse them. Make them think you are *one and the same.* 'Cuz you are.

—SHERMAN ATEN

Food for Thought

When children hear different messages from their parents, they key into the opportunity to use it to their advantage. Please don't ask us how that happens. It is instinctual and can make for difficulties in parenting.

Kids crave consistent messaging. They make bulk or fuss. But deep down, they know it represents stability in their home.

Review the situations below. Check which spouse is more lenient and then work together to meet somewhere in the middle for cohesiveness in responding to your children.

Which parent is more likely to "give in" regarding enforcement of the following family rules:

	DAD	MOM
• Staying out past curfew	____	____
• Completing household chores	____	____
• Eating all their food before dessert	____	____
• Getting good grades	____	____
• Attending church regularly	____	____
• Clearing their plate from the table	____	____
• Using sass or inappropriate talk	____	____
• Not respecting their elders	____	____
• Keeping their room clean	____	____
• Managing their laundry	____	____
• Practicing for sports, music, other lessons	____	____

THE VISION OF A BLESSED MARRIAGE

WALT DISNEY died during the construction of Disney World in Florida, and when it was completed and opened, a person said to one of Disney's top executives, "I wish Mr. Disney could have seen it!" The executive replied, "Oh, he did see it—that's why it's here!"

Do you have a God-inspired vision for your marriage? Since God is the One who originated the idea of marriage and He has much to say about it in the Bible, we would be wise to seek His perspective on what a blessed marriage looks like and how we can achieve it! It has been said that vision is a clear mental image of a preferable future imparted by God to His children. Because God loves us, He wants our marriage to be a meaningful journey, following His vision and blessing.

The Amplified Version of Proverbs 29:18 says, "Where there is no vision [no revelation of God and His word], the people are unrestrained." The New Living Translation says, "When people do not accept divine guidance, they run wild."

If you desire a healthy, strong, and rewarding marriage, base it on the vision, wisdom, and guidance that God alone can give you. Like Jesus responded to Satan when he told Him to turn stones into bread, "It is written: 'Man does not live on bread alone, but on every word that comes from the mouth of God." (Matthew 4:4)

If you haven't noticed, the world has all sorts of advice and temptations to try things their way. However, just like in the Garden of Eden, the tempter never tells you the rest of the story or the negative consequences of what appears so appealing! The apostle John was correct when he counseled us:

> *Do not love the world or anything in the world. If anyone loves the world, the love of the Father is not in them. For everything in the world—the lust of the flesh, the lust of the eyes and the pride of life— comes not from the Father but from the world. The world and its desires pass away, but whoever does the will of God lives forever.*
>
> 1 John 2:15-17 NIV

Therefore, our focus and vision must be on the Lord and His ways rather than the ways of the world. He designed marriage and will bless us as we keep our eyes on Him and seek to follow His directions.

When Jesus walked on the water toward the boat where His disciples were riding, they thought He was a ghost. He told them, "Take courage! It is I. Don't be afraid."

Peter said, "Lord, if it's you, tell me to come to you on the water."

Jesus said to him, "Come."

Peter got out of the boat and walked toward Jesus. But when he saw the wind, he was afraid and, beginning to sink, Peter cried out, "Lord, save me!" (Matthew 14:27 NIV)

We, too, must remember what Peter learned. Always keep our eyes on Jesus, trusting Him to lead us so that we may follow His vision for a beautiful and blessed marriage.

—GLENN WARD

Food for Thought

The word "vision" comes from the Latin "videre" and is defined as the ability to see something in the future with imagination and wisdom. Sharing a marriage vision between partners significantly strengthens a relationship. People walk toward what they see, so having a shared vision helps a couple walk directly toward that goal.

Goals are more likely reached when there is a vision behind them. For example, your goal may be to reduce debt. As a couple, you will walk toward that united vision because you "see" it together.

What visions have you created with your spouse for the future of your marriage? They could be centered around finances, health, career, family, travel, etc. List them below and intently give them to God each day in prayer.

Exercise your faith in these shared goals. Rather than thinking, "I'll believe it *when* I see it," try God's way: "I'll believe it *until* I see it!"

_____

_____

_____

_____

_____

_____

_____

_____

TOUCHING BASE

_____

_____

_____

_____

_____

_____

_____

WHAT EVERY MAN WISHES HIS WIFE KNEW ABOUT VALENTINE'S DAY

HOPEFULLY, the title here got your attention! Men, once you read this, you have my permission to make your wife read it. And I hope it helps.

February 14th is Valentine's Day, when love is celebrated, and couples honor each other. That-is-it! Ladies, it is not the litmus test of love. It is not proof that he loves you. It is not about the gift he gives or even about the gift he doesn't give.

It is not evidence that he knows or listens to you because you have been dropping "subtle" hints about what you want from him. It is not diamonds. Or flowers. Or expensive expressions of romance. (And guys, it's also not always Victoria's Secret!)

Many women enter into marriage with an attitude more closely resembling an 8th-grade girl than that of a grown woman!

- ✓ "He forgot about Valentines!"
- ✓ "He forgot my birthday!
- ✓ "That just proves how little I mean to him!"

No, it doesn't! It means that he failed your little pop quiz. It doesn't matter that he didn't *know* he was even taking a test!

It is not diamonds. Or flowers. Or expensive expressions of romance.

His love for you is based on how he stands with you and for you in life. Most people are so overwhelmed by life that the subtleties of hinting (seriously?) get lost in the glaringly bright light of reality!

I was once just as immature in my marriage as the women I'm describing. I wanted flowers, at least. And a handpicked card, too. Was that too much to ask? Could he not at least pretend to appreciate me that much? That monologue played in my head year after year.

Until the year when my dad had cancer. My days were full of keeping up with teenagers at home, caring for my mom after her heart surgery, and taking my dad from appointment to appointment with chemo chaos. When I was looking at my week on the calendar, I suddenly realized that the next day was Valentine's. I knew Jon was snowed under and somewhere in the Northwest, two time zones away (which does a number on you, too).

So, I picked up the phone and called him. I said, "Jon, tomorrow is Valentine's. I just realized it, so I wondered if you had realized the date."

"Oh no! It hadn't even crossed my mind," Jon replied, genuinely surprised. "What do you want?"

"I want the boys to know that Valentine's is important to recognize, so how about flowers? I can order them and pick them up between chemo treatments," I thought out loud.

"That sounds great."

I went further. "You usually get something for Hayley. Do you have anything in mind for her?"

He paused. "Yes, maybe a bear with balloons? Do you mind getting that too?"

"No problem. I can do that at the same time. What do you want my card to say, and what do you want on hers?"

We worked together to make every gift a success and make every recipient feel loved! That is the real point of marriage. It's not some ambiguous, passive-aggressive "test" of love, but working together to make everyone a winner. To make everyone successful. To give everyone in your family the knowledge that those you count on have your back.

That's love. Real, mature love. That a man would lay down his life for you . . . not that he reads your mind for Valentine's or your birthday. So grow up!

—KELLY RANDLES LANIER

Food for Thought

A cornerstone of marriage is honesty and openness. Hinting around for gifts or making veiled comments that aren't clearly expressed hinders communication. We shouldn't have to guess what our spouse needs or likes. And vice versa.

Ask for what you want. And ask them what they want. It may feel uncomfortable or intimidating initially, but it will ultimately lead to intimate communication between you.

And understand that change won't happen overnight. What can you do to help your spouse and children succeed in family matters? List three ways below:

1. _____

2. _____

3. _____

WHAT HAPPENS WHEN THE FAIRY TALE GETS REAL

Confess your faults one to another, and pray one for another, that ye may be healed. The effectual fervent prayer of a righteous man availeth much.

James 5:16 (KJV)

WHAT IS THE DIFFERENCE between a home shared with Jesus and one where He is a stranger? Prayer is the difference.

My first husband and I married straight out of college. We got good jobs and a new house and started our perfect life together. But, before two years were up, I found him with another woman. Our perfect life was shattered, and the man I had put on a pedestal came tumbling down. Since he wasn't perfect anymore, I divorced him without too much of a second thought. There was no forgiveness in me—just shock and betrayal.

I rushed into another marriage with a man who was a serial adulterer. The road to finding that out almost caused me to lose my mind. I questioned him often, and he always angrily replied that I was "crazy." My suspicions flooded my mind with doubt and guilt.

During this, I was driven to my knees. Oh, I had prayed throughout my life, but the prayers weren't earnest. Why should they be? Everything usually went my way.

Pain had never been a part of my life. But now, darkness had taken over—suffocating darkness. The expression about looking for the "light at the end of the tunnel" became very real. I was in a pitch-black tunnel, and there was no light anywhere. No way out.

My prayers were exhausting, and it felt as though I would drown in my sorrows. I prayed for God to show me I wasn't crazy. Although I sought a way out, that's not what I prayed for. Instead, I prayed for clarity and strength, and that's what I received.

God doesn't keep score.

God showed me all the proof needed that my husband was a liar and an adulterer, and He released me from guilt. Two and a half years after marriage #2, divorce #2 was now under my belt. I was on a roll and no doubt a disappointment to my family.

Believe it or not, I married once again. God heard my cry. My marriage is now in its 38th year. What's the difference now? Why did a two-time loser get another chance?

First, because God doesn't keep score. His mercies are indeed new every morning. And second, because my husband and I are doing something different. Jesus is now our first love. We both understand that we can't do this married thing alone. Each of us clearly remembers what it is like to walk without Jesus, and neither of us wants to return to that darkness.

So now, do I have a fairy tale life? *Not hardly.* But I thought Christians had perfect marriages. *Not hardly.* I thought Christians didn't argue at home. *Not hardly.*

Over the years, I have found that prayer for my husband has taken on many forms. I've prayed for healing when he is sick. I've prayed for guidance when he has decisions to make. But my favorite answers to prayers are the selfish ones I've made. *God has a sense of humor.*

After a disagreement and when we can't see eye to eye, my selfish prayers usually go like this, "God, please make my husband see it my way. Please, God, make him see how wrong he is and make him understand my side! Soften his heart!"

Without fail, the Holy Spirit moves, and the heart becomes soft. Except, it's always *my* heart first. Then, it's *my husband's* heart. And in asking God for my husband to see things my way, I begin to see things his way.

It's impossible to pray for someone earnestly and honestly without love. And it is the love of Jesus that makes the difference. Plenty of times, you will feel you don't love that partner you've been married to for what seems like a million years. So, since you don't love or even like him, how in the world can you pray for him?

If you are angry and confused about praying for a spouse, let me ask:

- ✓ Are you happy feeling the way you do?
- ✓ Are you tired of feeling sorry for yourself and your situation?
- ✓ Do you want your situation resolved?
- ✓ Have you already decided about how you want this situation to work out?
- ✓ Are you afraid the Holy Spirit will tell you something you don't want to hear?

You are just so angry, which may keep you from going to the Father and asking for anything. Maybe you think you must fix it before you ask for guidance. Satan has set up these roadblocks for you. And the hardened heart blocks that road inside you.

Where do you start? If need be, start with the selfish prayer I mentioned earlier. Getting it off your chest with the perfect Listener will help. If you pray selfishly over and over, don't give up. Keep talking. Over time, those conversations will become less angry, and as in any mediation, you will listen.

And then, the stone (your heart) will soften. Your attitude will soften. Your outlook will soften. Something new, perfect love, will fill the vessel (you). We will once again include love in the conversation.

You realize that you never would have gotten there alone. Love is the answer, and *prayer* is the difference.

—ALICE GILROY

Food for Thought

Prayer and the waiting that often comes with it can be exhausting. We feel our prayers are futile because we're just not seeing the answers, or the answers aren't what we're expecting.

If you feel exasperated about praying, you're not alone. Finding true peace through prayer can be affected by outside forces like stress, the demands of life, illness, etc. Like life itself, our prayer life goes through seasons: summer, spring, winter, and fall.

What "season" are you in currently with your prayer life? Was there a situation or circumstance that brought you there? Or was it just the living out of your days?

_____

_____

_____

_____

_____

_____

Be encouraged to persevere. In the heat of summer, there is always the assurance that fall is coming. Keep praying. It will get better. God is moving you along.

WHAT'S BEHIND THAT WALL?

Be sober, be vigilant; because your adversary the
devil, walks about like a roaring lion,
seeking whom he may devour.

I Peter 5:8 NKJV

POSSUMS. I don't know why they exist. When we were traveling full-time with our kids, we drove in late one night, parked our RV, and went into the house to head to bed. Immediately we exclaimed, "Eeeew! What is that stench?" We had no clue except that perhaps a rat had died in a wall. The smell was certainly too strong for a mouse. We promptly returned to our home on wheels and went to bed.

The next morning, upon entering the house, our dachshund made his way to our daughter's room and started sniffing the electric outlet. We then saw her baby picture on the wall pooching out. Ugh! There it was. Something hairy had exploded through the sheetrock right behind our little angel's baby picture. Yes, it was a possum—a recently pregnant possum!

The possum had found a nice dark place to have her babies, squeezing through a gap in our new roof where the flashing hadn't been replaced. And then she died. But her little hairy babies were all over our attic. Has this happened to anybody else!? I mean, really!?

Now, probably, there's more than one lesson to be learned here. First, check your roof flashings. I could have and should have done that myself.

And we are not to give the devil all the credit when things go crazy. However, the real lesson here is that, at times, we get ambushed from out of nowhere. I mean, is it a coincidence that the possum exploded out of the wall right on my daughter's picture? What are the odds? My daughter was and is still one of the most anointed worshippers I know. So that was just random? I think not! In fact, today, spiritual attacks on marriages and families are on steroids.

Husbands, dads, wives, and moms watch out for the invisible enemy. He's ruthless, and his stench is worse than the bloat they cut out of our wall. Also, don't think that you are always exempt because you love God and serve Him and His people. You and your family are even more of a target. If he can take you out, the domino fall has begun. He will find the opening where the flashing wasn't replaced or something you've ignored and do the unthinkable.

Maybe you know what is behind that wall in your marriage or family. And someone needs to cut it out and remove it. It's dead and has saturated areas you will need to fumigate and disinfect.

Please keep watch on your marriage and family and learn to recognize the fiery darts. They will come when you least expect them. Even when you're down and helpless, the devil knows no mercy and literally hates you. HE. HATES. FAMILY.

—SHERMAN ATEN

Food for Thought

This scripture for this devotion cautions that we must be sober or alert because our enemy wants to devour us. The word "devour" means to use up or destroy quickly. Devouring something is like a greedy fire ravaging a woodpile.

Being alert means keeping a careful watch or readiness for danger or opportunity. So, we can never back off or allow the enemy to have an occasion to attack us. It requires watchful prayer over your home and family.

Walk within each room of your home and pray the prayer below throughout. Be united with your mate in keeping watch over your household.

Dear Lord, your word declares that you are ever-present in our lives. As we walk through our home, we trust you to bless every space, every nook and cranny within these walls. We consecrate our home, our possessions, and our property to you, oh God. We are thankful for the angelic hosts divinely assigned to watch over us. We have faith that you are shielding our home, as you said in your Word, with a divine hedge of protection. To you be all the glory. In Jesus' name. Amen.

WHERE ARE YOU BUILDING YOUR HOME?

ONE OF THE MOST well-known literary pieces is commonly referred to as the *Sermon on the Mount,* and the speaker is Jesus Christ. It is a revolutionary teaching in which Jesus shows how a person can live effectively as a member of His Kingdom. Of course, it also gives excellent advice on how to have meaningful relationships in our families.

Jesus concludes the sermon with a call to commitment and a willful choice to positive action. In Matthew 7:24-29 Jesus described the choice of where we will build our home:

> *Therefore everyone who hears these words of mine and puts them into practice is like a wise man who built his house on the rock. The rain came down, the streams rose, and the winds blew and beat against that house; yet it did not fall, because it had its foundation on the rock. But everyone who hears these words of mine and does not put them into practice is like a foolish man who built his house on sand. The rain came down, the streams rose, and the winds blew and beat against that house, and it fell with a great crash. When Jesus had finished saying these things, the crowds were amazed at his*

*teaching, because he taught as one who had
authority, and not as their teachers of the law.*
Matthew 7:24-29 NIV

Nothing is said about the type of materials used in the construction of the house—only the location for the foundation upon which we build. He also says there will come storms with rain and wind beating on the structures. His point is that the key to surviving such assaults is the type of foundation one builds upon. Jesus also calls the builders either wise or foolish, depending on the foundation upon which they chose to build their homes. The wise person built his home on the solid foundation of the rock, while the foolish person built his on the sand.

As we build our homes, we can choose to be wise, making Jesus Christ and His Word the solid Rock foundation. Or we can carelessly and unwisely let the attitude and ways of the world be our pattern.

People have not really changed since the days when crowds gathered around Jesus to listen to him teach. Some heard and followed what He said. In contrast, others were merely curiosity-seekers who never really heard in a way that made any difference in their lives. Still today, some will hear a sermon or a teaching about Jesus and His Word and simply say, "That's nice," and go on about their lives unaffected by His Words. Others will truly hear His message and make the decision to build their home on the solid foundation of Jesus and His Word.

What about you? Is your home being built on the Rock, Jesus? Or is it being built "on the rocks"?

—GLENN WARD

Food for Thought

A proper foundation does more than support what is built upon it. It also protects, insulates, and resists shifting from the earth's movement. Likewise, a strong marriage is contingent on forming it on a solid foundation.

Compare the requirements for a firm, lifelong, physical foundation to the attributes of your marriage. What areas need to be strengthened?

A good foundation is:

- **Able to withstand several tons of weight.** Is your marriage strong enough to endure the pressure and shifts of the current day?
- **Level and plumb on all sides.** Is there an area in your relationship that has become out of balance?
- **Weatherproof against heavy storms.** Is your marriage strong enough to endure a downpour where the winds and waves beat against it? If not, what is needed to "shore up" the foundation and make it tempest-ready?

WHO ARE YOU SPEAKING WITH IN THE GARDEN?

A GARDEN is a beautiful place and a special place; it really hits our senses. We *see* the tremendous beauty of a rose; we *smell* its fragrance; we *touch* its delicate petals. We *hear* the wondrous sounds of birds singing or chimes hanging in a tree, making a beautiful sound. We *feel* the gentle breeze blow across our faces; it is a wonderful place to be still, reflect, pray, and know that he is God. And for me, it really tops it off while *tasting* a fabulous cup of coffee!

Now the Lord God had planted a garden in the East,
in Eden; and there he put the man he had formed.
Genesis 2:8-9 NIV

Then the Lord God made a woman from the rib he
had taken out of the man,
and he brought her to the man.
Genesis 2:22 NIV

They were in the garden **together.**

As Lori and I have been redoing our garden at the house, we realize there can also be danger in the garden. We encountered a few little snakes while moving some plants. Let's just say snakes are not Lori's favorite!

Adam and Eve encountered a snake in the garden as well but didn't recognize the danger associated with this serpent. Eve conversed with this snake, and she and Adam listened to what the serpent said in lieu of speaking and listening to the One who built that beautiful garden and placed them in it. They made a very poor choice and, as a result, plunged all of humanity into sin.

Jesus, on the other hand, spent time in a garden, the Garden of Gethsemane. In Matthew 26:36-46 Jesus took Peter, James, and John with him to pray. In verse 38, Jesus tells them, "Stay here and keep watch with me." And in verse 41, "Watch and pray so that you will not fall into temptation. The spirit is willing, but the body is weak." They didn't listen; they fell asleep.

Meanwhile, Jesus spoke and listened to the Father, praying several times, "My Father, if it is possible, may this cup be taken from me. Yet not as I will, but as you will." Adam and Eve spoke with the serpent in lieu of the Father and brought sin into our world. The disciples didn't pray to the Father and ended up deserting the Son of God. Jesus spoke with the Father and succeeded in saving humanity from sin and death.

Who are you speaking with in the garden? We have an enemy that seeks to steal, kill, and destroy our marriage and family. God's desire is for our marriage to flourish as it reflects the relationship between Christ and his bride the church. So, when we submit to God and resist the devil, he will flee from us.

Protect the garden of your marriage by being in constant communion with the One who created it.

—SCOTT & LORI DIX

Food for Thought

The latest trend in gardening involves the use of "low-maintenance" plants. But when we liken our marriage to a garden, we understand that it requires constant, ongoing care and nurture. There is no such thing as a maintenance-free marriage!

- Discuss the different ways the enemy tries to attack each of you. Ask yourself what your battle plan is for those attacks. Reference Ephesians 6:10-18.
- How are each of you intentionally caring for the garden of your marriage? In what ways have you been neglecting it? Pray and make any adjustments.
- Individually write down how you would describe your prayer life together. Is it non-existent? Poor? Sporadic? Solid? Great? Then, compare answers, discuss, and commit to improving now. In the words of a famous tennis shoe brand, "Just do it!"

Father, thank you for the gift of my spouse. May I care for them as you care for me. Show me how to tend to and keep the garden of our marriage so beautiful and rich that the sights, sounds, tastes, touch, and fragrance of our marriage please you. In Jesus' name. Amen.

WHY DO YOU LOVE ME?

LET'S REPLAY an ordinary conversation between couples:

Wife: "Honey, why do you love me?"

Husband: Thinks to himself, *Oh boy, here we go.*

Wife continues: "There are so many things I love about you—like your analytical mind, handsome eyes, and soft beard. Now, why do you love me?"

Husband: "Gee, how can I argue with that? Hmm. . . what do I say? [*awkward pause*] Well . . . I just love everything about you."

Wife: "No, you have to say something particular. You can't just say 'everything.'"

And so it goes! In some form or fashion, we have all had this conversation. One where our spouse asks us to express *why* and *how much* we love them. Is it that easy?

I am married to Kelly, one of the most beautiful people on earth. As of this writing, we have been married for only a few weeks. However, for 45 years, I was married to Sue, and for 38 years, Kelly was married to Jon. Our former spouses were the loves of our lives, and sadly, they both passed away.

At the time of their passing, our spouses were frail, yellow, bald, incoherent, and so, so tired. When they closed their eyes to this life, they had none of the physical, mental, emotional, or spiritual qualities we professed to love while on this earth. Yet, we loved them more than ever.

And so we ask, "Why do you love me?" Sometimes, I struggle with why God loves me. What is it He loves? I can think of nothing that deserves His love, no attribute that would compel it. I'm just not all that loveable.

Yet, I know He does. God loves me—warts and all — just because I am me. It isn't easy to comprehend that kind of love. But it is the same love Kelly felt for Jon and that I felt for Sue. And now we share that love for each other.

I love Kelly because she is Kelly. Yes, there are specific attributes that I particularly love about her, but we've both been there and done that. Our love for each other is something more significant than the sum of our two lives.

It's challenging to explain, and I'm not worthy of the task. As a sinner saved by grace and blessed by God's mercy, I have learned more fully how love works between a husband and a wife. And I'm grateful for that example as Kelly and I walk in marriage together. Maybe just saying a word of thanks and moving on with the responsibility of true love might be the godliest path to take.

And while walking with God and with her, I will continue to contemplate the question, "Why do you love me?" And Kelly will probably keep loving and, occasionally, ask me what I am thinking about.

Back to the top of the page we go!

—KIM LANIER

Food for Thought

It is often difficult to believe someone loves us because our thoughts and actions might not always be loveable. Or we might struggle with our sense of confidence or self-worth. So, finding someone who accepts all our warts, blemishes, and flaws can be truly amazing.

True love isn't a storybook romance or a fairy tale emotion. It is about committing to grow a love that will last. And lasting love comes when you know and understand that you are better *with* your spouse than without. It is achieved when you give without expecting in return, accepting their strengths and weaknesses.

Consider the ideas below as you commit to love your spouse in a way that will last your entire marriage:

✓ Share your hopes and dreams. Build exciting visions that your spouse can see themselves participating in and supporting.

✓ Express your appreciation for the ordinary tasks done every day without notice. Never take for granted that your spouse knows you're grateful. Say, "Thank you" for:

- Keeping the dishes washed.
- Filling our car up with gas.
- Sorting through the mail.
- Working hard to keep our family fed.
- Mowing the lawn or folding laundry, even when you're tired.

✓ Listen to your spouse rather than providing solutions to every problem. Turn off your cell phone and hear what they are saying.

Y'ALL PLAY NICE!

PART OF THE parent's mission is to teach their children to "play nice" with other children. This teaching involves sharing, not taking another child's toy if they are playing with it, and no name-calling, bullying, or ganging up. We want our children to learn to get along, right? Then why don't more married couples treat each other the same way?

In preparation for a move, my wife Dwaina and a friend were packing up the kitchen. I (Patrick) came into the kitchen to ask Dwaina a question. She politely answered. So, having the information I needed, I made my exit. As I left the kitchen, Dwaina's friend turned and asked, "Are y'all always that nice to each other?"

"Well, yeah," Dwaina replied, "most of the time, anyway." Her friend was shocked.

Not long after that happened, Patrick was meeting with a man. As Dwaina passed through the dining room, she patted Patrick's shoulder and asked if they needed anything. Again, after she left the room, the guest looked at Patrick and remarked, "Wow, that's unusual."

Patrick inquired, "What is?"

"The way you two just talked to each other. Is that normal for y'all?"

A passage in Ephesians teaches that how we talk to one another is really important! Here is how Paul lays it out to the Christians in Ephesus:

> *Do not let any unwholesome talk*
> *come out of your mouths, but only what is helpful*
> *for building others up according to their needs,*
> *that it may benefit those who listen.*
> *And do not grieve the Holy Spirit of God,*
> *with whom you were sealed for the day of*
> *redemption. Get rid of all bitterness, rage and*
> *anger, brawling and slander, along with every form*
> *of malice. Be kind and compassionate to one*
> *another, forgiving each other,*
> *just as in Christ, God forgave you.*
> Ephesians 4:29-32 NIV

These verses tell us that our words impact at least three relationships:

- ✓ Your relationship with the person you are speaking to (verse 29).
- ✓ Your relationship with those who hear how you speak (the last part of verse 29).
- ✓ Your relationship with God. Unwholesome words grieve the Holy Spirit of God (verse 30).

This passage gives us instructions for Christian Living. In verse 31, we are taught the things we must get rid of (i.e., eliminate) as part of our old sinful nature. And then verse 32 tells us what we need to practice in order to live as new people in Christ.

In summary, Y'ALL PLAY NICE!

—PATRICK & DWAINA SIX

Food for Thought

Becoming a person who plays well with others requires gaining some good attributes and relinquishing some poor ones. Compile a list of the things we are to give up, as written in Ephesians 4:31. Then note the things we are to live out, as expressed in verse 32.

As you compare the two lists, which items (good or bad) do you identify with the most? What needs to change?

Verse 31 says to put off:

_____

_____

_____

_____

_____

_____

Verse 32 tells us to:

_____

_____

_____

_____

_____

_____

YOU'RE GONNA MISS THIS

MARRIAGE AND FAMILY. It's God's wonderful plan and gift.

Our family grew up together, literally, 24 hours of every day!
We took togetherness to an entirely different level. LOL.
Church parking lots with our trailer . . . only one bathroom . . .
TOGETHERNESS.

The kids still laugh about "nap time" because they could barely move at the other end of the trailer.
And we would feel it . . . "KIDS! You're not sleeping!"
And you can run with that thought as a married couple in any way your imagination wants to go! LOL.

But what fun!
I wouldn't change a thing.
We saw the world together.
And we met a gazillion people!
We sang and ministered together . . . What a BLESSING!

- - - - - - -YOU'RE GONNA MISS THIS! - - - - - -

When Sherman and I were studying for our music degrees at Wayland University, I was focused on finishing my degree.

245

And I did!

But being from an educator family, my parents said, "Why don't you get that teaching certification, K-12? You'll never know where or when you might need it!"

Did I know God would call us full-time on the road as artists? No. But did He use my parent's wisdom? Yes!

When it came time to educate the kids, I was ready. I wouldn't change a thing.

I was blessed to hear them read for the first time. The one to see them do their first math problem.

- - - - - - -YOU'RE GONNA MISS THIS! - - - - - -

Gathered along 38 years of marriage, there are a few lessons and tips we want to share regarding family, kids, and even grandbabies.

1. **A family is not a Club but a Team.** The members:

Club	Team
Show up	Have the same goal in mind
Are always on their phone	Have the same purpose
Do different things	Connect daily
Have separate lives	Share a "unique" bond
Go here & there	Enjoy shared traditions
Think individually	Speak Y'all

2. **Bring them to Christ.** Take them to church. Read the Bible together and have devotions. Speak of God often and share what He is doing in your lives.

3. **Be present.**
   Stop cleaning and listen to that tall tale.
   Read that book.
   Play that game.
   Stop on the phone and computer.
   Throw that football or baseball.
   Play that game for the 100th time.
   Listen carefully.
   Be present.

- - - - - - -YOU'RE GONNA MISS THIS! - - - - - -

4. **Don't let your life or Christian walk contradict your words.** May they align. Are we perfect? No. But let them see you trying.

5. **Apologize.** Your kids will believe you're perfect while they're young. But as they grow, they will know you're not. Let them see you be real. Bow down. Ask for forgiveness when necessary.

6. **Keep a united front.** Be consistent with rules and discipline. Even when you disagree, have one plan of action in front of them.

7. **Work hard. Play hard.** Teach your kids a good ethic for work and play. This is a treasure key for their success in whatever they choose to do. Strive to teach them balance, which is only shown, not spoken.

8. **Remember that they learn how to do marriage and family from the two of you!** Model that. Date your spouse in front of them.

9. **Teach them about priorities.**
   o God is first.
   o Spouse is second.
   o Kids are third.
   Many couples have this all in the wrong order!

So many couples tell us they:
- Never saw their parents fight, so they didn't know how to resolve conflict. Resolve conflict in front of your children in a healthy way!

- Never saw their parents be affectionate. Ever.
  As a couple:
  HUG,
  KISS,
  DANCE IN FRONT OF THEM.
  WATCH THEM SCREAM,
  SQUEAL,
  AND JUMP IN THE MIDDLE!

10. Nothing puts a sense of security in your little ones more than when they observe that mom & dad *like* and *love* each other. Show them every day!

And finally, don't you dare blink . . . because . . .

- - - - - - -**YOU'RE GONNA MISS THIS!** - - - - - -

—TAMMY ATEN

Food for Thought

The Bible says we learn and grow from the experiences of others. Work to implement the tips of excellent advice provided in this devotion from a seasoned marriage. Be blessed as you integrate these ideas into your family.

ABOUT THE AUTHORS

Sherman & Tammy Aten have been serving God in a full-time itinerant calling since November of 1990. Many know them as worship leaders and the founders of Three2One Marriage. God has given the Atens a hunger for authentic worship in the Body of Christ & a passion for Godly marriages & families.

They ministered with their son, Josh & daughter, Brooke, as The Aten Family, leading worship in over 2000 churches of all denominations and in 14 countries. Today, they spend an average of 30 weeks per year ministering as a couple in the U.S. & internationally.

A special focus of Three2One Marriage is on pastors & wives. God has allowed them to minister to these servants in Ukraine,

Pakistan, Portugal, Spain, Venezuela, and recently underground pastors & wives brought into Turkey.

Sherman presently serves as a Trustee for Wayland Baptist University, their alma mater, where they studied music together. Tammy began her piano studies at North Texas State before transferring to WBU, where she completed her Bachelor of Music Education degree.

They are certified "Together in Texas" pre-marital counselors and trained as Prepare & Enrich facilitators. Presently, they serve on staff at Acton Baptist Church in Granbury, Texas, where they make their home and ministry base.

But most importantly, they have four granddaughters: Jennah (with an "h"!), Charlee (Daniels!), Presley Jo Leigh & the newest addition, Miss Kinna Blair.

CONTRIBUTORS

Patrick and Dwaina Six have been married for 40 years, and they have two adult children and one granddaughter. They live in Amarillo, TX. Patrick has re-careered after 36 years of church ministry in Texas and  Oklahoma—as a Senior Pastor and as a Family Minister. He is now preparing the next generation of Christian leaders at a Christian Academy where he teaches Bible. Dwaina helps people be good stewards of their finances as a Financial Advisor. They have led marriage ministry events all over the US and abroad since 1993.

 **Lennie and Alice Gilroy** are retired and live at Lake LBJ in Kingsland, TX. They married in 1985 and have one son, a daughter-in-love, and two grandchildren. The couple has spent their working careers as police officers and newspaper publishers. They have worked side by side as police officers in Houston, Floyd County, and Austin. For 23 years, Alice was publisher and editor of the Floyd County newspaper, with Lennie also helping out in productions and deliveries as well as serving as County Commissioner. They have served on the board for Aten Ministries for over 30 years.

Believing that marriage is our second strongest testimony, **Bobby and Margie Manthei** have helped facilitate marriage renewals in North America, Central America, South America, and Eastern Asia. Bobby recently retired as a public and government affairs leader in the Natural Gas and Oil industry. Margie holds a lifetime Texas Superintendent Certification and retired as a school administrator. Her educational career includes high school English teacher, educational diagnostician, and guidance

counselor. Their three grandchildren, Maren, Samuel, and George, motivate them to stay young and seek adventure. Bobby & Margie presently live in Aledo, TX.

Ed and Elizabeth Plants live in Kirkwood, Missouri, and have been married for 40 years. They have six grown children and one granddaughter. Ed is the pastor of Geyer Road Baptist Church. Elizabeth is a college and high school math teacher. They are experienced speakers at marriage conferences across the US and have been on Aten Ministries' Board of Directors for over 30 years.

Scott and Lori Dix: Scott is a Bi-vocational Pastor and Associate Pastor at Waples Baptist Church in Granbury, Texas. He also works as a Systems Engineer Principal at Lockheed Martin in Fort Worth. Lori serves as a Wee School Teacher at Acton Baptist Church in Granbury. They have three beautiful daughters named Jennifer, Alyssa, and Brianna. They also have a son-in-law named Tyler Cole and three precious grandchildren named Hunter, Cooper, and Aubrey.

Glenn and Carolyn Ward reside in Richardson, TX. But Glenn was born in Abilene, Texas, and grew up in Anson, Vega, and Snyder. He worked at the Permian Basin Baptist Encampment and met Carolyn Springer during the summer after he graduated from high school. Two years later, they were married and graduated from Hardin-Simmons

University. Glenn served churches in Anson, Ft. Griffin, and Clyde, in west Texas, before going to First Baptist Church, Acton, near Granbury, where he served as pastor for over 37 years. Upon retirement, he served as the Director of Missions for the Paluxy Baptist Association for eleven years. Carolyn taught school for sixteen years before retiring. She also has two life callings: 1) supporting women who live with mental illness (as she does), and 2) encouraging women in ministry. They have three daughters, two sons-in-law, and two grandchildren.

Dr. Joe and Nancy Stewart live in Seminole, Texas, where Joe serves as Lead Pastor of First Baptist Church in his 35th year of vocational ministry. Nancy is a talented musician and interior decorator and serves in marriage conferences domestically and internationally. They are celebrating 42 years of marriage and have three daughters and five grandsons.

God allowed **Kim and Kelly Lanier** to hit the marriage jackpot twice! Kim was a School Superintendent for almost 40 years. He was happily married to his high school sweetheart, Sue, and looking forward to his retirement years with her. Sue was diagnosed with pancreatic cancer on Kim's first day of retirement and passed away six months later. Kelly Randles was married to her high school sweetheart for 38 years. Her husband, Jon, was an incredible pastor and evangelist who saw thousands come to Christ during his vast ministry. Jon decided to come "off the road" as a traveling evangelist and become Lead Pastor at Victory Life Church in Lubbock, Texas. Within a few months of their move to Lubbock, he was diagnosed with pancreatic cancer. Jon preached every Sunday until the very end, nine months later. The Randles/Lanier clan is now blended into nine adult kids, 17 grandkids, and one great-grandchild! Kim and Kelly live in Mustang, Oklahoma, with their Frenchie, Gus.

Marshall & Brooke (Aten) Cochrum were married in January 2020 and presently serve as Youth Pastors at His Place Fellowship Church in Paris, Texas. Marshall, a former college basketball player & MMA fighter (yes, he's 6' 9"), is living his dream as a youth minister and coach. He coaches basketball & also teaches self-defense at a Christian school. His wife, Brooke Aten, graduated from Dallas Baptist University with a Music Business degree and joined the staff at Fielder Church in Arlington, Texas. She became an integral part of worship, co-leading & co-writing with the worship pastor & team. But now, probably best of all, they have given the Atens (Poppi & Gigi) their 2nd biological granddaughter, Miss Kinna Blair Cochrum!

MINISTRY CONTACT INFORMATION

To schedule a conference or inquire about bulk pricing for this book, please use the contact details below:

Aten Ministries • PO Box 5925 • Granbury, TX 76049
atenmin@gmail.com

Website: www.a10s.org

Facebook: Aten Ministries
             Three2One Marriage Conferences